Guggenheim
Museum

etropolitan
useum of Art

Whitney Museum
of American Art

Frick
Collection

UE

useum of
odern Art

MIDTOWN
MANHATTAN

fth
venue

Chrysler
Building

Grand
Central
Terminal

mpire State
uilding

Carl
Schurz
Park

Roosevelt
Island

East

on

Gramercy
Park

GRAMERCY PARK
HISTORICAL
DISTRICT

nion
quare
Park

EAST
VILLAGE

NOHO

Tompkins
Square Park

East
River
Park

Hamilton
Fish Park

O

TAN

LITTLE
ITALY

LOWER
EAST SIDE

Seward
Park

Corlears
Hook
Park

CHINATOWN

Columbus
Park

Rutgers
Park

City
all Park

East

WALL
STREET

South Street
Seaport

Jeanette
Park

Ellis Island &
Statue of Liberty

D0431577

CITYPACK TOP 25
New York

KATE SEKULES

If you have any comments
or suggestions for this guide
you can contact the editor at
Citypack@theAA.com

AA Publishing
Find out more about AA Publishing and the wide
range of services the AA provides by visiting our
website at www.theAA.com/travel

How to Use This Book

KEY TO SYMBOLS

🕂 Map reference to the accompanying fold-out map

✉ Address

☎ Telephone number

🕓 Opening/closing times

🍴 Restaurant or café

🚆 Nearest rail station

Ⓜ Nearest subway (Metro) station

🚌 Nearest bus route

⛴ Nearest riverboat or ferry stop

♿ Facilities for visitors with disabilities

❓ Other practical information

▷ Further information

ℹ Tourist information

✋ Admission charges: Expensive (over $9), Moderate ($3–9), and Inexpensive ($2 or less)

⭐ Major Sight ★ Minor Sight

👣 Walks

🚌 Excursions

🛍 Shops

🎵 Entertainment and Nightlife

🍴 Restaurants

This guide is divided into four sections

• **Essential New York:** an introduction to the city and tips on making the most of your stay.
• **New York by Area:** We've broken the city into six areas, and recommended the best sights, shops, entertainment venues, nightlife and restaurants in each one. Suggested walks help you to explore on foot.
• **Where to Stay:** the best hotels, whether you're looking for luxury, budget or something inbetween.
• **Need to Know:** The info you need to make your trip run smoothly, including getting about by public transportation, weather tips, emergency phone numbers and useful websites.

Navigation In the New York by Area chapter, we've given each area its own color, which is also used on the locator maps throughout the book and the map on the inside front cover.

Maps The fold-out map accompanying this book is a comprehensive street plan of New York. The grid on this fold-out map is the same as the grid on the locator maps within the book. We've given grid references within the book for each sight and listing.

Contents

CONTENTS

Introducing New York

"New York is an island off the coast of Europe." Your Manhattan friends have been quoting this well-used witticism more than ever since the 2004 presidential election. A mere 16.6 percent of Manhattanites voted for Bush.

Of the so-called Blue States—those dominated by Democrats—New York is the bluest of them all. The qualities that weld New Yorkers to the city also mark them out as alien to heartland America. Residents of Manhattan value directness, diversity and creativity; they live at a ridiculous pace; they work all hours (they have to, to feed the mortgage); they walk—fast—everywhere; they fail to keep their opinions to themselves; they have street smarts; they are capital L Liberal. The city that actually lived through the attack that kicked off this era of paranoia and xenophobia, refuses to give into fear; New Yorkers have all the *chutzpah* they ever did.

Not that the city hasn't changed. Here, where some hip neighborhood is forever preparing to eclipse the last hotspot, change is the only constant. The crime-ridden, graffiti-scarred mean streets of the late 20th century are but a distant memory. In fact, terrorist threats notwithstanding, New York remains the safest large city in America, according to the FBI Uniform Crime Report. In stark contrast to the gritty days, you'll see Bugaboo strollers everywhere, because there is a mini baby-boom in progress. Real estate prices are in the realm of fiction, and a whole lot of regular folks, especially creative types, have decamped for Brooklyn, while those who can't afford Brooklyn have gone to Queens. Harlem is all glamorous and beautiful; the Bronx is next. Staten Island, the fifth borough that most visitors know only for its fabulous ferry is the final frontier. Since, in Richmond County, a whopping 56.7 percent of voters pulled the lever for Bush in 2004, that frontier may not be broached for a long while yet.

Facts + Figures

- **Visitors in 2005: 41 million (a record)**
- **Dollars spent by visitors: $22 billion**
- **Hotel rooms by end 2007: 75,000**
- **New restaurants per year (average): 60**

REAL ESTATE

The obsession with real estate here easily rivals that of the UK. With prices rising continually and bubble fears—at least as we go to press—failing to materialize, the homes of many property-owning New Yorkers are not just their castles, they are their portfolio, retirement plan and chief financial burden.

BROOKLYN

Once a separate city, the vast borough across the East River has seen a migration of disaffected New Yorkers that has changed it forever. Once Brooklyn was unfashionable; now it's a Manhattanite's night-time destination for restaurants, music and parties in those oh-so-desirable brownstones.

SMOKING

In October 2002 then-new mayor Michael Bloomberg dealt a radical blow to the tobacco industry—and some say to the city's bars—by banning smoking in all workplaces. The reception of such a sweeping piece of legislation was mixed at first, but smoke-free bars and restaurants seem quite normal now. The consensus: a Good Thing.

A Short Stay in New York

DAY 1

Morning Begin your day at 8.30 by taking the subway to **Grand Central Terminal** (▷ 58) and having breakfast in the splendid food court. Looking at the main hall as you pass slowly through, then exit at 42nd Street and walk east to the **Chrysler Building** (▷ 52). Swing into the lobby, continue east through Tudor City to United Nations Plaza and walk north.

Mid-morning Stroll around the UN gardens by the East River, then take a tour of the **UN General Assembly Hall** (▷ 66). Double back on 42nd Street to Fifth Avenue and look in at the **New York Public Library** (▷ 61).

Lunch If it's summer, get something from the very good kiosks in Bruant Square or sit at one of Bryant Park Café's outdoor tables. In bad weather, eat inside the main restaurant.

Afternoon Walk a block and a half up Avenue of the Americas to the **International Center of Photography** (▷ 65) and after a quick viewing, head another block west to **Times Square** (▷ 63). Explore there, then join a line at the TKTS booth for discounted Broadway tickets.

Mid-afternoon Take Seventh Avenue up to 37th Street and go east, passing through the diamond district, to **Rockefeller Center** (▷ 62). Look around, then continue north up Fifth Avenue, passing St Patrick's Cathedral to your right. For the rest of the afternoon, either shop **Fifth Avenue** (▷ 56) or head to **MoMA** (▷ 60) half a block west on 53rd Street. Or, if neither appeals, keep going up Fifth to **Central Park** (▷ 74).

Dinner Take up your early reservation at swanky **Lever House** (▷ 70).

Evening Enjoy whichever show your scored discount tickets for.

Morning Have a light breakfast at **Café Sabarsky** (▷ 88) in the Neue Galerie and be at the **Metropolitan Museum of Art** (▷ 80) when it opens at 9.30. Spend the rest of the morning exploring the galleries.

Mid-morning Go back to the **Neue Galerie** (▷ 84), which opens at 11, and then squeeze in the Guggenheim. (Not ideal but at least you'll get a taste.)

Lunch Head over to Madison Avenue to **Jackson Hole** (▷ 88) for a burger, or if it's a beautiful day, leave enough time to enter Central Park at 85th Street and have lunch at the **Boat House** (▷ 88).

Afternoon Take the downtown 6 from 86th Street to Spring Street and do some shopping in Soho. If shopping's not your thing, stay on the 6 (crossing the platform at Brooklyn Bridge, City Hall to the 4, 5) to Bowling Green, walk through Battery Park and board a ferry to the **Statue of Liberty** (▷ 26) and **Ellis Island** (▷ 25).

Dinner Dine at **Café Gray** (▷ 70) in the Time Warner Center, enjoying the view of the city lights. Or if you thought far enough ahead, take your place at **Per Se** (▷ 70). If you did the latter, that *is* your evening.

Evening Walk up Broadway to **Lincoln Center** (▷ 94). If it's summer, take your dancing shoes to Midsummer Night's Swing on Josie Robertson Plaza; if not watch a performance in one of the many halls. Afterwards, take in the late session at **Dizzy's Club Coca Cola** (▷ 99) back at Time Warner.

Shopping

Thought there was nothing you couldn't buy over the internet? Think again! New York is a shopping haven, with clothing, furniture, food and souvenirs available no place else. Shopping is still one of the best ways to get an inside look at life in New York—its trends, fads, pace, cultural influences and sense of humor. From massive department stores to small boutiques, the city has something for everyone.

A Piece of New York
You'll find all kinds of NYC paraphernalia—from Statue of Liberty coin banks and taxicab neckties to sweatshirts bearing the New York Police Department initials and Yankee baseball caps. Museum shops offer reproductions, posters, jewelry, stationery and commemorative items.

Fashion
For fashion head for Nolita and Soho, where small (and often expensive) boutiques line the streets. Major franchises can also be found here, along Broadway, and side streets such as Prince Street, Broome Street and Spring Street. If you're planning a night out on the town, try the stores along 8th Street, starting on Broadway and heading west. These are popular among young clubbers—mannequins in the storefronts flaunt outrageously sexy garb.

Music
Music lovers will find no shortage of places to

Shoes in a Soho shop; sweet bread in Union Square; designer label in Chelsea; happy shopper

---

WINDOW SHOPPING

No visit here is complete without window shopping. Start on Lexington between 59th and 60th streets: You'll see the flags outside Bloomingdale's. Walk west to Madison Avenue; between 60th and 61st streets is Barney's, for expensive clothing, jewelry, accessories and beauty products. Walk west along 57th Street, past Chanel and Christian Dior, to the prestigious Henri Bendel and Bergdorf Goodman stores. On Fifth Avenue peer in at Gucci, Tiffany's and Prada.

browse, whether looking for chart-toppers or something from the past. CDs are available at major chain stores such as Tower Records and Virgin. In the Village, smaller music stores carry vintage records, tapes and CDs at prices ranging from a few dollars to several hundred for collectors' editions. Note: DVDs and videos cannot be played on European machines.

Bargains

If you are looking for a bargain, try the popular sample sales, where designer brands are marked down as much as 80 percent. Designer sales are often held at open showrooms over a few days. Arrive early on the first day of the sale for the best selection, though prices do drop as days go by. To learn about sample sales pick up *New York* magazine or *Time Out New York*, or log onto www.dailycandy.com or www.nysale.com. For electronic goods try Best Buy (✉ 60 W23rd Street ☎ 212/366-1373) or Circuit City (✉ 52 W14th Street ☎ 212/387-0730, plus other locations).

A Bite to Eat

As for food, in addition to the many upscale restaurants and cafés, simple NYC classics like hot dogs, pizza, bagels and frozen yogurt can be found on nearly every street corner, along with food carts purveying anything from hot soft pretzels or candied almonds to six kinds of curry or falafel sandwiches—great street food that can't be beat after a long day of shopping.

East Village outlet; Kors on Mercer Street; Dean & Deluca deli; glassware; Macy's at Christmastime

FLEA MARKETS

Bric-a-brac is at a premium in New York, where everything has the potential to show up on a movie set. What was the city's main flea market (✉ Around 25th and 26th streets) running every weekend has been truncated by the construction of residential blocks, and could disappear. For the time being, the indoor market down the street (✉ 112 W25th Street) remains open on the weekends. Uptown, check out GreenFlea markets on Saturdays (✉ 44 Columbus Avenue).

Shopping by Theme

Whether you're looking for a department store, a quirky boutique, or something in between, you'll find it all in New York. On this page shops are listed by theme. For a more detailed write-up, see the individual listings in New York by Area.

CLOTHES

Abercrombie & Fitch
  (▷ 32)
Barneys (▷ 45)
Bergdorf Goodman
  (▷ 68)
Betsey Johnson (▷ 97)
Brooks Brothers (▷ 32)
Calvin Klein (▷ 85)
Canal Jeans (▷ 32)
Cynthia Rowley (▷ 32)
Donna Karan (▷ 85)
Henri Bendel (▷ 32)
Jeffrey NY (▷ 45)
Jeffrey Loehmann's
  (▷ 45)
Malia Mills (▷ 97)
Marc Jacobs (▷ 45)
Moschino (▷ 85)
Paul Smith (▷ 45)
Ralph Lauren (▷ 85)
Resurrection (▷ 32)
Shanghai Tang (▷ 85)
Scoop (▷ 45)
Steven Alan (▷ 97)

DISCOUNT

Century 21 (▷ 32)
DSW and Filene's (▷ 45)
Ina (▷ 32)

SHOES

Barneys (▷ 97)
DSW (▷ 85)
Manolo Blahnik (▷ 68)

FOOD AND WINE

Chelsea Market (▷ 45)
Fairway (▷ 97)
Gourmet Garage (▷ 32)
Greenmarket (▷ 45)
Kam Man Foods (▷ 32)
Whole Foods Market
  (▷ 68)
Zabar's (▷ 97)

DEPARTMENT STORES

Barneys (▷ 45)
Bergdorf Goodman
  (▷ 68)
Bloomingdales (▷ 85)
Macy's (▷ 68)
Saks (▷ 57)
Takashimaya (▷ 68)

BOOKS

Barnes and Noble (▷ 97)
Kitchen Arts and Letters
  (▷ 85)

HOMEWARE

ABC Carpet & Home
  (▷ 45)
Butter & Eggs (▷ 32)
Crate & Barrell (▷ 85)
Fish's Eddy (▷ 97)
Michael C. Fina (▷ 68)
Pearl River Mart (▷ 32)

STATIONERY

Kate's Paperie (▷ 45)

SPORTS GOODS

Nike Town NY (▷ 68)
Patagonia (▷ 87)

BEAUTY

Zitomer (▷ 85)

MISCELLANEOUS

Alphabets (▷ 97)
FAO Schwartz (▷ 68)
Lunettes et Chocolat
  (▷ 32)

ACCESSORIES

Coach (▷ 68)
Laila Rowe (▷ 97)

New York by Night

As the sun sets over New York, the city becomes at-once a sultry, romantic and mysterious place. Wander through Times Square as the glitzy electric billboards pop out from the dark sky. A stroll, run or bike ride along the pedestrian path on the banks of the Hudson River on the West Side offers a spectacular view of the sunset and the Jersey shore.

Nightlife
Clubs and restaurants come to life after dark. As young New Yorkers explore new frontiers in the city, the Meatpacking district—once known for drugs and prostitution—has become home to trendy bars and clubs. Celebrity sightings are common at Spice Market (✉ 403 W13th Street ☎ 212/675-2322) and 5 Ninth (✉ 5 9th Avenue ☎ 212/929-9460). At the other end of the spectrum are biker bars like Hogs-n-Heiffers (✉ 859 Washington Street, at W13th Street) and The Village Idiot (✉ 355 W14th Street at 8th/9th Avenues), friendly dives where the beer flows cheaply and the music blares loudly.

Take to the Water
Circle Line Cruises' evening boat rides around Manhattan are a relaxing way to see the world's most famous skyline. Board at Pier 83, at 42nd Street on the Hudson River (☎ 212/563-3200). Tour guides on board explain the legends of the city (☎ 212/563–3200).

FOR A LAUGH
Comedy clubs are a great way to sample New York's sense of humor. Venues such as Caroline's (✉ 1626 Broadway, at 50th Street ☎ 212/757–4100), Upright Citizens Brigade Theater (✉ 307 W26th Street, between 8th and 9th ☎ 212/366–9176) and Stand Up NY (✉ 236 W78th, at Broadway ☎ 212/595– 0850) are popular. Gotham (✉ 208 W23rd Street between 7th and 8th Avenues ☎ 212/367–9000) has even been known to host surprise visits from Jerry Seinfeld.

Bright lights of Times Square and clubbers enjoying New York's nightlife

Eating Out

You can dine around the world in New York City. Some New Yorkers dine out every night, others save the top-class choices for special occasions. Dining trends change from season to season.

Plan Ahead
It's wise to make a reservation for dinner, especially on weekends. Indeed, top-class restaurants always require reservations. If you want a table at Jean-Georges, Le Bernardin, Per Se or similar, call well in advance. Sometimes it can be tough to get through even to the reservationists. Just keep trying. You may be able to eat at the bar in one of these fancy restaurants. In Midtown, luncheon reservations are also often essential. Very few places still require a jacket and tie at dinner so ask when making a reservation. In general, casual smart is the way to go.

Vegetarian Options
Many of the top-class dining rooms offer vegetarian menus, and even fast-food joints are offering more healthful options on their menus these days.

When to Go
Breakfast may be served all day at coffee shops and diners, but usual breakfast hours are from 7 to 11am. Lunch usually runs from noon to 2.30pm and dinner from 5pm to 11pm. Many restaurants offer brunch on weekends.

TAXES, TIPPING AND FINANCIAL MATTERS
A sales tax of 8.65 percent will be added to your dining bill. The minimum tip (with good service) is 15 percent; many people double the tax for a 17.3 percent tip. Many restaurants offer prix fixe menus, which are good value. In January and late June, a special promotion offers a three-course menu for $20.12 (luncheon) or $35 (dinner) at numerous restaurants; this promotion is often extended so it's always worth checking if it's available.

Eating an ice cream; Costa Azzurra in Little Italy; hot dog; café at South Street Seaport; bagels

ESSENTIAL NEW YORK EATING OUT

Restaurants by Cuisine

There are restaurants to suit all tastes and budgets in New York. On this page they are listed by cuisine. For a more detailed description of each restaurant, see New York by Area.

CLASSIC

Le Bernardin (▷ 70)
Café des Artistes (▷ 100)
Café Boulud (▷ 88)
Chanterelle (▷ 34)
Daniel (▷ 88)
Del Posto (▷ 48)
Gramercy Tavern (▷ 48)

CLASSIC NY

Boat House (▷ 88)
Four Seasons (▷ 70)
Katz's Deli (▷ 34)
Odeon (▷ 34)
Oyster Bar (▷ 70)
Peter Luger (▷ 108)
Tavern on the Green (▷ 88)
Serendipity 3 (▷ 88)
'21' Club (▷ 70)
Union Square Café (▷ 48)

CONTEMPORARY

Blue Ribbon (▷ 108)
Café Gray (▷ 70)
Gotham Bar and Grill (▷ 48)
Grocery
Jean-Georges (▷ 100)
Lever House (▷ 70)
The Modern (▷ 70)
Per Se (▷ 70)
Thor (▷ 34)

ASIAN

Jing Fong (▷ 34)
Nobu (▷ 34)
Osaka (▷ 108)
Sushi of Gari (▷ 108)
Yama (▷ 48)

CASUAL

Barney Greengrass (▷ 100)

Boat Basin Café (▷ 100)
Bubby's (▷ 108)
Carmine's (▷ 100)
Jackson Hole (▷ 88)
Juniors (▷ 108)
Katz's Deli (▷ 48)
Lombardi's (▷ 34

EUROPEAN

Al di La (▷ 108)
Aix (▷ 100)
Café Sabarsky (▷ 88)
Ouest (▷ 100)
Pace (▷ 34)
Picholine (▷ 100)
The Red Cat (▷ 48)
Sherwood Café (▷ 108)

COMFORT FOOD

Bette (▷ 48)
Schillers (▷ 34)
Spotted Pig (▷ 48)

If You Like...

However you'd like to spend your time in New York, these top suggestions should help you tailor your ideal visit. Each sight or listing has a fuller write-up in New York by Area.

STAR CHEFS

Jean Georges Vongerichten's Jean Georges (▷ 100) is the flagship of his ever-growing world-wide empire.
Daniel Boulud at Daniel will wow you (▷ 88). Don't forget the madeleines.
Good luck scoring a table at Per Se (▷ 70). Thomas Keller has been called the best chef in America. Often.
For fish, nobody beats Le Bernadin's (▷ 70) Eric Ripert.

STAYING HIP

Trot over to Jeffrey New York (▷ 45) to refresh your wardrobe, or for vintage, Resurrection (▷ 32).
Get a taste of the LES at the Parkside Lounge (▷ 33).
Have a late supper at The Spotted Pig (▷ 48).
Bed down at 60 Thompson (▷ 114), The Gansevoort (▷ 114) or, if broke, Hotel QT (▷ 111).

TO PARTY TILL DAWN

O Bar is a scene, especially the garden in summer (▷ 46).
Slow it down for a couple of frames at Amsterdam Billiards (▷ 99), open till 4am.
Blue Ribbon is at its busiest late (▷ 108).
NYC's best cheesecake at 3am? Juniors! (▷ 108)

Enjoy the best that New York has to offer—a lot of it is free!

A ROOM WITH A VIEW

Harbor rooms at the Ritz Carlton Battery Park (▷ 114) come complete with telescope.

Take in the lovely lake view from Central Park's Boat House (▷ 88)— unique in Manhattan.

Not everyone knows about the Iris and B. Gerald Cantor Roof Garden (▷ 86) at the Met.

If you're not staying at Beekman Tower (▷ 112), visit the 26th floor restaurant/bar.

Do you even need to be told about the Empire State Building (▷ 54).

BRINGING THE KIDS

FAO Schwartz (▷ 68) is more than a store—especially since the renovation.

They won't believe the five-story indoor ferris wheel at Toys R Us, Times Square (▷ 63).

You can never go wrong with a zoo. Bronx Zoo is vast (▷ 106); the one in Central Park (▷ 74) won't take all day.

Take them to Serendipity 3 (▷ 88) for frozen hot chocolate.

Get tickets for the New Victory Theater (▷ 69).

CLASSIC NYC

See the ceiling, covered in toy trucks at the clubby 21 Club (▷ 70).

Bergdorfs, Saks and Bloomies are classic department stores with different personalities (▷ 68, 57, 85).

Buildings too countless to mention. Start with the Chrysler (▷ 52).

See how the other half lived at the Frick (▷ 77) and Cooper-Hewitt (▷ 76).

SPORTING PURSUITS

Hope you're here in baseball season (April to September; postseason to October). Yankee Stadium (▷ 107) is a must. Or catch the Mets at Shea.
Madison Square Garden has it all (▷ 65, 69): basketball (the Knicks), boxing, tennis, track and field…
There's a game of something in progress in Central Park (▷ 74) all summer long. If it's winter, you can skate at Wollman Rink.
Shop for outdoor sports at Patagonia (▷ 97).

A LAUGH

Caroline Hirsch broke Jerry Seinfeld, Tim Allen and Rosie O'Donnell. Twenty-something years on her club, Caroline's (▷ 69), still rocks.
A non-grungy stand-up venue: Gotham Comedy Club (▷ 46).
Score free tickets for a taping of Conan O'Brien or the *Daily Show* with Jon Stewart.
Go see the Tom Otterness sculptures on the A, C, E, 14th Street platform.

EATING WHERE IT'S AT

Thor is a showcase for people as well as Kurt Gutenbrunner's food (▷ 34).
To spot models, try Schiller's (▷ 34) late.
Amy Sacco runs the best nightclubs, and now a restaurant too. Head for Bette (▷ 48).
All Mario Batali's places are hotspots; his fanciest by far is Del Posto (▷ 48).
Taste a little of the Brooklyn scene at Sherwood Café (▷ 108).

There is always so much to see and do and enjoy in New York

New York by Area

$11.50 /LB
特價 $48.50 /LB磅
特大宗谷元貝碎
$ 36.
日本宗
江瑤

The cradle of New York, Lower Manhattan has bags of history—new citizens in the 19th century first landed here—as well as the financial district, the historic seaport district and iconic Statue of Liberty.

Around Lower Manhattan

18

19

20

21

22

23

Clarkson   Street
Washington   Street
HOUSTON   STREET
Houston   Street
VARICK   STREET
AVENUE OF THE AMERICAS (6TH AVENUE)
Prince   Street
WEST   Prince   Street
King   Street
WEST STREET   Charlton   Street
Vandam   Street
HUDSON STREET   Spring   Street
Spring   Street
GREENWICH STREET   Dominick   Street
New York City Fire Department Museum
Broome   Street
Sullivan   Street
Thompson   Street
West Broadway   Wooster   Street
Greene   Street
Mercer   Street
SOHO
St Patrick's Old Cathedral
Prince   Street
Little Singer Building
Spring   Street
Haughwout Building
Spring   Street
Mott   Street
Mulberry   Street
Crosby   Street
LITTLE ITA
kenmare
Broo

HOLLAND TUNNEL
WEST STREET
Watts   St
Renwick St
Spring   St
Hudson St
Watts   Street
Desbrosses   Street
Vestry   Street
Laight   Street
VARICK   Canal   Grand   Street
CANAL   STREET
Howard   Street
Canal   Street
Tony Shafrazi Gallery
Children's Museum of the Arts
BROADWAY
Grand   Street
Canal   Street
Baxter   St
Centre   Market P.
Mulberry   Street
Lispenard   Street
Canal   Street
Beach   Street
LOWER MANHATTAN
Walker   Street
White   Street
Franklin   Street
Museum of Chines in the America
white   Street
Bayard
Columbus Park
Hogan Place

19

LAIGHT   STREET
Ericsson Place
Beach   Street
Hubert   Street
North Moore   Street
Franklin   Street
Franklin   Street
FRANKLIN   STREET
CHURCH   STREET
Harrison   Street
TRIBECA
Leonard   Street
Worth   Street
Thomas   Worth   Stre
Paine   Park
Foley   Square
Pearl   Street
US Courthouse
Thomas   Street
Duane   Street
Jay St
Staple St
BROADWAY
Trimble Pl
Reade   Street
Cardinal   Street

20

Washington Market Park
GREENWICH STREET
Duane   Street
Reade St
CHAMBERS
Chambers   Street
STREET
Chambers   Street
City Hall
Brooklyn Bridge - City Hall
PARK
Av
BROOKL

Warren   Street
Warren   Street
WEST   STREET
Murray   Street
City Hall
City Hall Park
City Hall and Civic Center
PARK ROW
Spruce   Street
BROOKL

Park Place West
Park Place
Murray   Street
Park   Place
Woolworth Building
Beekman   Street
Spruce   Street

21

BATTERY PARK CITY
Barclay   Street
9A
BARCLAY   Street
Vesey   Street
VESEY STREET
CHURCH   STREET
Church of St Peter
VESEY ST
Ann   Street
Broadway Nassau St
Fulton   Street
Park Row

St Paul's Chapel
Fulton   St
Fulton Street
Dey   Street
Fulton   Street
John   Street
Fulton   Street
WILLIAM

Ground Zero
Cortlandt   Street
Cortlandt Street
Cortlandt   Street
MAIDEN   LANE
American Numismatic Society
Platt   St

Liberty   Street
Liberty   Street
Liberty   Street
Federal Reserve Bank
Liberty   Street
Cedar   Street
MAIDEN
Fletc

WEST STREET
Albany   Street
Washington Street
Cedar   Street
TRINITY   Pine   Street
Trinity Church
Federal Hall National Monument
WALL   Street
Wall   Street
WALL STREET

22

Rector   Street
South End Avenue
Rector   Street
Rector   Place
Rector   Street
New York Stock Exchange
Broad   Street
Exchange   Place
NEW   Street
BROADWAY
OLD SLIP
New York City Police Museum
Fletc

Hudson
West Thames Street
Little   West Thames   Street
1st   Place
Museum of American Financial History
Morris   Street
Morris   Street
GREENWICH STREET
Beaver   Street
Stone   Street
SOUTH   STREET
Jeanette Park
Couver

2nd   Place
Bowling Green
Battery Place
Bowling Green
Fraunces Tavern Museum
Whitehall Street
STATE STREET
Vietnam Veterans PLAZA

Museum of Jewish Heritage
Robert F Wagner Jr Park
Battery Place
Rectory of the Shrine of Elizabeth Ann Seton
PETER MINUIT PLAZA

0   300 m
0   250 yds
Battery Park
Castle Clinton
Admiral George Dewey Promenade
HIGHWAY 9A
Staten Island Ferry Terminal

Ellis Island & Statue of Liberty
BROOKLYN BATTERY TUNNEL

C   D   E

New Museum of
Contemporary Art

Lower East Side
Tenement Museum

Bowery

BOWERY

STREET

Grand
Street

Grand

BOWERY

STREET

Elizabeth
Street

Street

Bell Street

Division

East
Broadway

James
Place

Oliver
Street

Catherine
Street

Madison

Mills
Road

of the
Finest

BRIDGE

Dover
Street

Peck Slip

Beekman

Street

Fulton Street
Market

Chrystie

Forsyth

Eldridge

Allen
Street

Orchard
Street

Ludlow
Street

Essex
Street

Norfolk
Street

Suffolk
Street

Clinton
Street

Attorney
Street

Ridge
Street

Pitt
Street

Rivington Street

Street

DELANCEY

STREET

Essex
Street

Delancey
Street

LOWER
EAST SIDE

WILLIAMSBURG   BRIDGE   APPROACH

Ridge   Street

Willett   Street

Columbia   Street

Lewis

Broome

Street

Broome   Street

Grand

Street

Orchard
Street

Ludlow
Street

Street

Norfolk
Street

Ludlow

Seward
Park

Hester

Canal

Street

Division
Street

Pike

East   Street

Broadway

Clinton

Jefferson St

Rutgers

Madison

Monroe   Street

Clinton

Street

Gouverneur
Street

Montgomery

Jackson Street

Street

Street

Street

Water

CHINATOWN

East

Henry

Broadway

Market
Street

Monroe   Street

Cherry   Street

Pike

Monroe St

Catherine

Street

Market

Clinton   Street

Rutgers   Park
South

Jefferson Street

Gouverneur
Street

Rutgers
Park

Montgomery
Street

FRANKLIN   DELAND   ROOSEVELT   DRIVE

MANHATTAN   BRIDGE

East

BROOKLYN   BRIDGE

SOUTH STREET

South Street
Seaport

F

G

H

Chinatown

Streetlife in Chinatown (left and below)

THE BASICS

➕ F20

✉ Roughly delineated by Worth Street/East Broadway, the Bowery, Grand Street, Centre Street

🍴 Numerous (some close around 10pm)

🚇 J, M, Z, N, R, 6, A, C, E, 1, 9 Canal Street; B, D Grand Street

🚍 M1, B51

♿ Poor

❓ General tours

☎ 212/465-3331; NYC Discovery Tours

HIGHLIGHTS

● Buddhist temple (✉ 64B Mott Street)
● Chinatown History Museum (✉ 70 Mulberry Street)
● Pearl River Mart (✉ 477 Broadway)
● Doyers Street: once the "Bloody Angle"
● Columbus Park (✉ Bayard/Baxter streets)

New York's Chinatown has swallowed nearly all of Little Italy and has spread over a great deal of the Lower East Side. Wander here and you're humbled by the sight of a lifestyle that thrives.

Going west Chinese people first came to New York in the late 19th century, looking to work for a while, make some money and return home. But, by 1880 or so, some 10,000 men—mostly Cantonese railroad workers decamped from California—had been stranded between Canal, Worth and Baxter streets. Tongs (sort of secret mafia operations) were formed, and still keep order over some 150,000 Chinese, Taiwanese, Vietnamese, Burmese and Singaporeans. New York, incidentally, has two more Chinatowns: in Flushing (Queens) and 8th Avenue, Brooklyn, with a further 150,000 inhabitants, but Manhattan's is the world's largest.

A closed world Although you may happily wander its colorful streets, you will never penetrate Chinatown. Many of its denizens never learn English and never leave its environs. The 600 factories and 350 restaurants keep them in work; then there are the tea shops, mah-jong parlors, herbalists, and the highest bank-to-citizen ratio in New York, in which Chinese stash their wages (normally not more than $10,000–$20,000 a year) to save for the "eight bigs" (car, TV, DVD player, fridge, camera, phone, washing machine and furniture), to send home, or eventually to invest in a business of their own.

Ellis Island at night (below); a Circle Line ferry passing Ellis Island (right)

Ellis Island

This museum offers a humbling taste of how the huddled masses of new immigrants were not allowed to go free until they'd been herded through these halls, weighed, measured and rubber stamped.

Half of all America It was the poor who docked at Ellis Island after sometimes grueling voyages in steerage, since first-class passage included permission to decant straight into Manhattan. Annie Moore, aged 15 and the first immigrant to disembark here, arrived in 1892, followed by 16 million founding fathers over the next 40 years, including such then-fledgling Americans as Irving Berlin and Frank Capra. Half the population of the United States can trace their roots to an Ellis Island immigrant.

Island of Tears The exhibition in the main building conveys the indignities, frustrations and fears of the arrivals. (As you arrive, collect your free ticket for the half-hour film, *Island of Hope/Island of Tears*, or you'll miss it.) You are guided around more or less the same route new arrivals took: from the Baggage Room, where they had to abandon all they owned; onward to the large Registry Room, now bare of furniture; and through the inspection chambers where medical, mental and political status were ascertained. The Oral History Studio brings it all to life as immigrants recount their experience—especially moving when coupled with the poignant items in the "Treasures from Home" exhibit. This is a demanding few hours' sightseeing. Wear sensible shoes and bring lunch.

THE BASICS

✚ Off map at E23
✉ Ellis Island
☎ 212/363–3200
🕐 Daily 9.30–5, closed 25 Dec
🍴 Café
Ⓜ 4 Bowling Green, then take ferry
🚌 M1, M6, M15, then take the ferry
🚢 Ferry departs Battery Park South Ferry every 40 minutes. Ferry information ☎ 212/269–5755
♿ Good
💵 Inexpensive
❓ Audio tours available

HIGHLIGHTS

● Wall of Honor
● Treasures from Home
● Oral History Studio
● Dormitory
● Augustus Sherman's photos
● View of Lower Manhattan

Statue of Liberty

HIGHLIGHTS

- View from the pedestal
- Statue of Liberty Museum
- Fort Wood, the star-shape pedestal base
- Her new centenary flame

TIP

- A visit to the Statue of Liberty can be combined with a trip to Ellis Island since most ferries stop at both islands.

The green lady, symbol of the American dream of freedom, takes your breath away, however many times you've seen her photograph—and despite her surprisingly modest stature.

How she grew   In the late 1860s, sculptor Frédéric-Auguste Bartholdi dreamed of placing a monument to freedom in a prominent location. His dream merged with the French historian Edouard-René de Laboulaye's idea of presenting the American people with a statue that celebrated freedom and the two nations' friendship. Part of the idea was to shame the repressive French government, but, apparently, New Yorkers took their freedom for granted: It was only after Joseph Pulitzer promised to print the name of every donor in his newspaper, the *New York World*, that

Clockwise from left: Tourists posing at the base of the Statue of Liberty; Liberty seen on her island; detail of one of the most famous statues in the world; a coin-operated look-out point for viewing the Statue of Liberty

the city's citizens coughed up the funds to build the pedestal. Liberty was unveiled by President Grover Cleveland on October 28, 1886.

Mother of exiles Emma Lazarus' stirring poem, *The New Colossus*, is engraved on the pedestal, while the tablet reads: July IV MDCCLXXVI—the date of the Declaration of Independence. Beneath her size 107 feet, she tramples the shackles of tyranny, and her seven-pointed crown beams liberty to the seven continents and the seven seas.

What is she made of? Gustave Eiffel practiced for his later work by designing the 1,700-bar iron and steel structure that supports her. She weighs 225 tons, is 151ft (46m) tall, has an 8ft (2m) index finger and a skin of 300 copper plates. The torch tip towers 305ft (93m) above sea level.

THE BASICS

www.nps.gv/stli

✚ Off map at E23

✉ Liberty Island

☎ 866/782–8834 or 866/269–5755

◷ Daily 8.30–5. A limited number of daily tickets to tour the monument may be reserved in advance from ferry office or by phone

🍴 Cafeteria

🚇 4 Bowling Green, then take ferry

🚌 M1, M6, M15 South Ferry, then take ferry

🛥 Ferry departs Battery Park South Ferry (AF19). Ferry information

☎ 212/269–5755

♿ Poor

🎫 Inexpensive

South Street Seaport

TOP 25

The skyline behind the seaport (left); entertainment for visitors (below)

THE BASICS

www.southstseaport.org

🌐 F21

✉ Visitor center: 12 Fulton Street. Tickets also from Pier 16

☎ 212/748–8600

🕐 Jun–end Sep Fri–Wed 10–6; Oct–end May Fri–Wed 10–5. Closed Dec 25 and Jan 1

🍴 Numerous

🚇 1, 2, 4, 5, J, M, Z Fulton Street; A, C Broadway/ Nassau Street

🚌 M15 Pearl/Fulton Street

♿ Poor

💲 Inexpensive

HIGHLIGHTS

● View of Brooklyn Heights
● Richard Haas' Brooklyn Bridge mural
● Late forays in the Fulton Fish Market (midnight–8am)
● Boarding *Andrew Fletcher*
● Titanic Memorial
● Chandlery
● Fulton Market (especially the bakeries)

This reconstructed historic maritime district, with its cobbled streets, is a tourist trap. However, when you stroll the boardwalk on a summer's night, with the moon over the East River, you are very glad to be a tourist.

Pier, cruise, shop, eat The seaside/cruise-ship atmosphere is what's fun at the Pier 17 Pavilion, which juts 400ft (122m) into the East River, overlooking Brooklyn Heights. It's a mall, with chain stores, bad restaurants and a food court, but also three stories of charming wooden decks. The adjoining piers, 16 and 15, harbor a number of historic vessels with picturesque arrangements of rigging, as well as the replica side-wheeler, *Andrew Fletcher* and the 1885 schooner, *Pioneer*, which give harbor cruises. Your cash is courted by many stores, housed in the 1812 Federal-style warehouses of Schermerhorn Row—Manhattan's oldest block—and around Water, Front and Fulton streets, and by the cafés in the old Fulton Market.

Many museums The Seaport Museum Visitors' Center acts as clearing house for all the small-scale exhibitions here. One ticket admits you to: the second-biggest sailing ship ever built, the Peking; the floating lighthouse, Ambrose; the Children's Center; the Seaport Museum Gallery; a re-creation of a 19th-century printer's shop; various walking tours (including "Ship Restoration" and "Back Streets"—worthwhile if you have the time) and more.

More to See

BATTERY PARK
This refuge for workers in the Financial District, was named for the cannon sited here to defend the fledgling city against British attack. Buy tickets for the Statue of Liberty at Castle Clinton, a national monument.
➕ E23 ✉ Tip of Manhattan Ⓜ A, C, J, M

CHILDREN'S MUSEUM OF THE ARTS
Highlights include the Monet Ballpond, Architects Alley and the Wonder Theater.
➕ E18/19 ✉ 182 Lafayette Street ☎ 212/941–9198 🕐 Wed, Fri–Sun noon–5, Thu noon–6 Ⓜ 6 Spring Street ✋ Inexpensive

CITY HALL
French Renaissance-style facade and elegant Georgian interior—see it by visiting the Governor's Room, with a small furniture museum.
➕ E20 ✉ Broadway (Murray Street) ☎ 212/788–3000 🕐 Mon–Fri 10–3.30 Ⓜ 2, 3 Park Place; 4, 5, 6 Brooklyn Bridge/City Hall; N, R City Hall ✋ Free

GROUND ZERO
The exact nature of the building that will replace the Twin Towers, destroyed by terrorists on 9/11 remains undecided at this writing, though completion is estimated at 2011.
➕ D21 ✉ Church to West streets, Liberty to Vesey Streets Ⓜ M6, M9

LOWER EAST SIDE TENEMENT MUSEUM
This reconstruction of life in an 1863 tenement block is a must for history buffs. Intriguing tours and talks.
➕ G18 ✉ 90 Orchard Street ☎ 212/431–0233 🕐 Tue–Fri 1–3.30, Sat–Sun 11–4.30 Ⓜ F, J, M, Z Delancey Street; B, D, Q Grand Street ✋ Moderate

NEW MUSEUM OF CONTEMPORARY ART
What MoMA stops at, Whitney shows; where Whitney balks, this museum starts.
➕ F18 ✉ 583 Broadway (Houston/Prince streets) ☎ 212/219–1222 🕐 Wed–Sun noon–6, Sat noon–8 Ⓜ N, R Prince Street ✋ Inexpensive

A poignant tribute at Ground Zero

World Trade Center Globe Statue Memorial, Battery Park

AROUND LOWER MANHATTAN ★ MORE TO SEE

NEW YORK CITY POLICE MUSEUM

A small museum with a wealth of cops and robbers material including handguns, uniforms and shields. You can visit a prison cell and learn about forensics. The NYPD Hall of Heroes includes a memorial to the policemen and women who died on 9/11.

🏠 F22 ✉ 100 Old Slip ☎ 212/480–3100 🕐 Tue–Sat 10–5 🚇 N, R, 2, 3 💰 Donation suggested

NEW YORK STOCK EXCHANGE

The neoclassical facade dates only from 1903. The Stock Exchange is not currently open for visits or tours. Telephone for up-to-date information about possible opening.

🏠 E22 ✉ 20 Broad Street ☎ 212/656–5167 🚇 2, 3, 4, 5 Wall Street; J, M, Z Broad Street 💰 Free

ST. PATRICK'S OLD CATHEDRAL

New York's first Roman Catholic cathedral opened in 1815. At that time, the area was settled by Irish immigrants. The original structure was destroyed in a fire in 1866, but enlarged and rebuilt by 1868. When the new St Pats was built in 1879, the cathedral became a parish church.

🏠 F18 ✉ 260–64 Mulberry Street 🚇 N R, Q

SINGER BUILDING & HAUGHWOUT STORE

Two of the best ambassadors for the Soho Cast Iron Historic District —the 26 blocks of skyscraper forerunners, now galleries and upscale boutiques. The Haughwout had the first Otis steam elevator.

🏠 E18 ✉ Singer: 561 Broadway. Haughwout: 488 Broadway 🚇 N, R Prince Street; F, S Broadway/Lafayette

WOOLWORTH BUILDING

The world's tallest until the Chrysler, Cass Gilbert's Gothic beauty has NYC's richest lobby—see the witty bas reliefs of Gilbert and tycoon F. W. Woolworth. It now contains condos.

🏠 E21 ✉ 233 Broadway 🕐 Lobby Mon–Fri 7–6; closed holidays 🚇 2, 3 Park Place; N, R City Hall

Woolworth Building

Interior of St. Patrick's Old Cathedral

Downtown

A stroll through the highlights of downtown.

DISTANCE: 2 miles (3km) **ALLOW:** 40 minutes

START

CHURCH STREET
🚇 Park Place 1, 2

END

GREENWICH VILLAGE ▷ 40
🚇 W4th Street A, B, C, D, F, V

1 Walk east on Barclay Street, turn left on Broadway and look to your left for the Woolworth Building. At City Hall Park turn left onto Broadway, where City Hall comes into view on your right.

2 Walk east through the park and catch a vista of Brooklyn Bridge. Continue north up Centre Street to Cass Gilbert's US Courthouse on Foley Square.

3 The neoclassical New York County Courthouse is past Pearl Street on the right, and then, past Hogan Place, the Criminal Courts (The Tombs).

4 Another block, and here's Canal Street. Go east to Mulberry Street. Continue north through Little Italy and veer west on Prince Street to the Cast Iron Historic District of Soho.

8 Keep heading west to expore the Village further.

7 Fifth Avenue starts at the north side. Look at gated Washington Square Mews (first right), turn left on W 8th Street (see MacDougal Alley, first left) to Avenue of the Americas (6th Avenue).

6 Take any route west through the streets of Soho, heading north across Houston Street anywhere from Mercer to MacDougal; now you're in Greenwich Village. Three blocks north, you reach Washington Square, the center of New York University.

5 Look at the Singer Building opposite as you cross Broadway.

AROUND LOWER MANHATTAN

WALK

31

Shopping

ABERCROMBIE & FITCH
Teens and college grads are the core customers at this temple to slouchy American style, famous for its rather racy Bruce Weber-shot catalogs. The clothes, though, are good for anyone's weekends and the prices are gentle. There are men's and women's lines.
🚇 E21 ✉ 199 Water Street/Fulton Street
☎ 212/809-9000 🚇 2, 3, 4, 5, A, C, J, M, Z Fulton Street–Broadway/Nassau

BROOKS BROTHERS
Home of the preppy, Brooks Brothers also caters to anyone, male or female (though the men's department is way better) who wants to look pulled together. Their basics, like boxer shorts and white dress shirts are exceptional.
🚇 E21 ✉ 1 Church Street/Liberty Plaza
☎ 212/267-2400 🚇 R, W Cortlandt Street

BUTTER & EGGS
This beautifully laid-out store stocks the kind of accessories that adorn its multimillion-dollar loft neighbors: modern classic housewares of all types, including multitudes of multicolor pillows in rich silks.
🚇 E20 ✉ 83 West Broadway/Warren Street
☎ 212/676-0235 🚇 1, 2, 3, Chambers Street

CENTURY 21
Practically a cult, especially in the European designer area.
🚇 E21 ✉ 22 Cortlandt Street ☎ 212/227-9092
🚇 N, R City Hall

CYNTHIA ROWLEY
Adorable, hip dresses and shoes. Shop here for a night out on the town.
🚇 E19 ✉ 112 Wooster Street
☎ 212/334-1144 🚇 N, R Prince Street

GOURMET GARAGE
The place to find yellow cherry tomatoes, dried cherries, fresh clams, truffle butter, smoked duck, gelati, you-name-it.
🚇 E18 ✉ 435 Broome Street (Mercer Street)
☎ 212/941-5850 🚇 N, R Prince Street

PEARL RIVER MART
Shop here for chrome lunch pails with clip-on lids; embroidered silk pajamas and Suzy Wong dresses; bamboo fans and porcelain rice bowls–all the things, in fact, you can get in the smaller Chinatown emporia, but collected under one roof. The food department sells an eclectic range. The prices are very, very low.
🚇 E18 ✉ 477 Broadway (Broome Street) ☎ 212/431-4770 🚇 N, R Canal Street

INA
Showroom samples and barely worn designer duds. The prices are high, but fair; there's a men's version round the corner.
🚇 E18 ✉ 21 Prince Street
☎ 212/334-9048 🚇 N, R Prince Street

KAM MAN FOODS
This large Chinese food store overflows with exotic products, from live fish and edible bird's nests to ginseng priced at hundreds of dollars. It also sells inexpenisve Asian cookware.
🚇 F19 ✉ 200 Canal Street at Mott Street ☎ 212/571-0330 🚇 J, M, Z Canal Street

LUNETTES ET CHOCOLAT
Owner Selima Salaun's barmy notion of combining the most fashionable eyewear with handmade chocolates somehow works at this charming Nolita boite.
🚇 F18 ✉ 25 Prince Street (Mott Street) ☎ 212/925-8800 🚇 6 Spring Street

RESURRECTION
A haul of pricey but perfect vintage, with an emphasis on collectible labels: Pucci, Halston, Courrèges, Dior et al. The owners also offer their own line of skirts and tops.
🚇 F18 ✉ 217 Mott Street between Spring and Prince streets ☎ 212/625-1374
🚇 6 Spring Street

Entertainment and Nightlife

BOWERY BALLROOM
This venue lets the alternative musicians spread out a bit. It is indeed like a ballroom, with a proscenium arch stage.
➕ F18 ✉ 6 Delancey Street (Bowery) ☎ 212/533-2111 Ⓜ J, M Bowery, 6 Spring Street

BLARNEY STAR
Some big name traditional Irish musical entertainers perform her on Friday nights.
➕ D21 ✉ 43 Murray Street ☎ 212/732-2873 Ⓜ N, R, W City Hall

BRIDGE CAFÉ
"Café" is a misnomer for this loveable place that's been serving continuously since 1794—yes it's one of the oldest taverns in town. The restaurant is OK, but the bar is a lovely place to end an evening after a stroll by the water.

COCKTAIL CULTURE
Cocktail culture is alive and well in the Big Apple. The martini craze is here to stay—many lounges and bars offer long menus of creative concoctions. Elegant glassware is crucial. Atmospheres range from urban chic to clubby lounge to pubs.

Neighborhood pubs, with more emphasis on beer and bourbon, are favorite watering holes. Or, instead of alcohol, visit one of New York's coffee bars.

➕ F21 ✉ 279 Water Street/Dover Street ☎ 212/227-3344 Ⓜ 4, 5, 6 Brooklyn Bridge/ City Hall

DOUBLE HAPPINESS
The first lounge bar in Chinatown, this trendy subterranean cocktail den pays homage with Asian tchotchkes (count the abacuses…) and green-tea martinis. Not for quiet conversation.
➕ F18 ✉ 173 Mott Street ☎ 212/941-1282 Ⓜ 6, N, R, Canal Street

THE KNITTING FACTORY
The Main Space, the KnitActive Sound Stage, the Old Office and the Tap Bar are the four performance rooms at the leading venue for new music. In the basement is a lounge.
➕ E20 ✉ 74 Leonard Street (Church Street/ Broadway) ☎ 212/219-3055 Ⓜ 1, 9 Franklin Street

PARKSIDE LOUNGE
A multipurpose venue that hosts live music, stand-ups, karaoke, and people kicking back with a beer after a long day—or night. It's open until 4am. An unpretentious minimally art-directed place to sample the Lower East Side buzz.
➕ Off map at H18 ✉ 317 Houston Street/Attorney Street ☎ 212/673-6270 Ⓜ F, V 2nd Avenue

RISE
The cocktail area of the Ritz-Carlton is not your typical hotel bar.
➕ D23 ✉ 2 West Street at Battery Place, 14th floor ☎ 917/790-2626 Ⓜ 4, 5 Bowling Green

S.O.B.'S
The Latin beat keeps you dancing at this tropically themed nightclub ("Sounds of Brazil"). Also African, reggae and other island music.
➕ D18 ✉ 204 Varick Street ☎ 212/243-4940 Ⓜ 1, 9 Canal Street

TONIC
Lower East Side hipsters cram into this dive for techno via songsters to straight-up jazz.
➕ G18 ✉ 107 Norfolk Street (Delancey/Rivington streets) ☎ 212/358-7503 Ⓜ F Delancey Street

KEEPING UP
One of New York's favorite pastimes is keeping up with what's on. Look for extensive weekly listings in the magazines *New York, Time Out New York* and *New Yorker*, or the Friday and Sunday editions of the *New York Times*. You can also pick up free copies of the *Village Voice* and *New York Press* newspapers in storefronts and vestibules around town. The monthly listings in *Paper* magazine have a decidedly downtown focus.

Restaurants

PRICES

Prices are approximate, based on a 3-course meal for one person.
$$$ over $60
$$ $40–$60
$ under $40

CHANTERELLE ($$$)
Serene restaurant on a quiet Tribeca corner. Billowy curtains, flower arrangements and elegant tables provide the perfect backdrop for a romantic evening. The seafood sausage is a dream.
➕ D20 ✉ 2 Harrison Street/Hudson Street ☎ 212/966-6960 🕐 Closed Sun, Mon lunch 🚇 1, 9 Franklin Street

JING FONG ($)
An unmissable dim sum experience: Trolleys laden with everything from steamed pork buns to stewed chicken feet whizz through an enormous room—hail them before the best bits go.
➕ F19 ✉ 20 Elizabeth Street /Bayard and Canal streets ☎ 212/ 964-5256 🕐 Go before 3pm 🚇 6, N, R Canal Street

KATZ'S DELI ($)
The site of the hilarious climactic scene in When Harry Met Sally is the last remaining deli in what was a thriving Jewish neighborhood. Opened in 1888, it upholds traditions: nondescript surroundings and knishes and pastrami sandwiches.

➕ G18 ✉ 205 East Houston Street ☎ 212/254-2246 🚇 F, V Lower East Side/2nd Avenue

NOBU ($$$)
It is difficult to get a reservation at this Japanese shrine but you'll be rewarded by the hauntingly delicious food. The dining room is a modern Japanese fantasy with lots of bamboo. Choose from baby abalone, live scallops, or sashimi drizzled with garlic and ginger-infused olive oil.
➕ D19 ✉ 105 Hudson Street/Franklin Street ☎ 212/219-0500 🕐 Closed Sat, Sun lunch 🚇 1, 9 Franklin Street

PACE ($$)
A beloved restaurateur duo have brought to life this huge Tribeca room,

ODEON ($$)
After celebrating its quarter-century in 2005 with all the '80s faces that made it the first hotspot of the Bright Lights Big City age, this art deco-style restaurant still outdoes half the new boîtes in town. Its tiled floors, dim lighting, happy bar area and open-most-hours welcome are some reasons why—that and the always-reliable nouvelle-American cooking.
✉ 145 West Broadway/Thomas Street ☎ 212/233-0507 🚇 A, C Chambers Street

serving an equally huge menu of snob-rustic Italian food that New Yorkers have taken to their hearts (thanks, largely, to Mario Batali): crudi; panini; risotto; stuffed wild boar; veal chop; and sugar-dusted zeppoles.
➕ D19 ✉ 212 Hudson Street/North Moore ☎ 212/965-9500 🚇 1, 9 Franklin Street

SCHILLERS ($–$$)
The latest hit from the man who brought faux-France to Manhattan (Balthazar, Pastis) veers toward the Mitteleuropa-slash-deli model. It's quite a scene, though off hours tend to be peaceful and pleasant.
➕ Off map at G18 ✉ 131 Rivington Street/Norfolk Street ☎ 212/260-4555 🕐 Closed Sun, Mon lunch 🚇 F, V Delancey Street

THOR ($$$)
The name is an acronym for the high-design hotel that houses it. As if to match the fabulous Marcel Wanders design, Austrian chef Kurt Gutenbrunner waxes more creative here than at his three other NY places: butter-poached lobster with cherries or white tomato mousse are the kind of dishes on the small-plate menu.
➕ Off map at G18 ✉ The Hotel on Rivington, 107 Rivington Street/Essex Street ☎ 212/796-8040 🚇 F, V Delancey

Below 14th Street find the East Village and Soho where everything from high-fashion stores to ethnic restaurants and bohemian bars to bijou theaters are open (almost) all hours.

East Village

HIGHLIGHTS

● Sidewalk artists and book stalls
● Polish-Ukrainian restaurant, Veselka

TIP

● For a calm break, head to Tompkins Square Park, bordered by Avenues A and B, between 7th and 10th Streets. Once the very definition of "needle park," it couldn't be nicer now, with fresh plantings and children frolicking on the lawns.

Once for those priced out of Greenwich Village, East Village is now expensive bohemia and what used to be the edgiest "nabe" in town is now a youthful playground of restaurants and boutiques with a smattering of historic sights.

Early days The area was settled by Dutch, Irish, German, Jewish and Ukrainian immigrants between 1800 and 1900. By 1830, the Vanderbilts, Astors and Delanos were among those who lived in grand houses on Lafayette Street.

Notable buildings Cooper Union, founded by engineer Peter Cooper and built by 1859 is a designated landmark and it was here that Abraham Lincoln made his famous anti-slavery speech. West

Clockwise from top left: Typical East Village buildings; two carved lions at the entrance to the church of St. Marks in the Bowery; a colorful delivery vehicle; Astor Place; walking the streets; a decorated building

of St Mark's Square is the Gothic Revival Grace Church, built in 1846 by James Renwick Jr. Renwick was also responsible for the federal-style Stuyvesant-Fish House, built in 1803 for Peter Stuyvesant who gave it as a wedding present to his daughter and Nicholas Fish. The Ukrainian Museum is an introduction to the cultural heritage of the Ukrainians who settled here. The displays include decorated Easter eggs, ritual cloths, costumes and a lot more.

Literary appeal A haunt of the Beat poets in the 1960s, East Village attracted Allen Ginsberg, Andy Warhol, Timothy Leary and many radicals. Today the area has its artists and literary types, as well as holding a great appeal to visitors. The range of budget ethnic restaurants and smart eateries offers plenty of choice for lunch.

THE BASICS

✚ F16; east of Bowery and south of 14th Street
Ⓕ F Second Avenue; 6 Astor Place

Ukrainian Museum
www.ukrainianmuseum.org
✚ F17
✉ 222 East 6th Street (2nd and 3rd Avenues)
☎ 212/223-0110
🕐 Wed–Sun 11.30–5
💵 Moderate

Greenwich Village

TOP 25

The Row (left); Washington Arch (middle); Jefferson Market Library (below)

THE BASICS

➕ C17

✉ East–west from Broadway to Hudson Street; north–south from 14th Street to Houston Street

🍴 Numerous

🚇 A, C, E, B, D, F W4th Street; 1, 9 Christopher Street

🚌 M10

🚆 PATH Christopher Street

♿ Poor

HIGHLIGHTS

● Cafés and jazz clubs
● Washington Square Park
● NYC's narrowest house (75 Bedford Street)
● West (of Hudson Street) Village
● Halloween Parade
● Jefferson Market Library
● Citarella and Jefferson Market (food stores)
● Minetta Lane

This sugar-sweet, picturesque, human-scale neighborhood of brownstones and trees is one of the romantic images of Manhattan, familiar from sitcoms and movies. Its dense streets are rewarding to wander and you can take a break in a café or jazz club.

What village?   It was named after Greenwich, southeast London, by the British colonists who settled here at the end of the 17th century. In the 18th and early 19th centuries the wealthy founders of New York society took refuge here from smallpox, cholera and yellow fever.

Bohemia, academe, jazz   When the elite moved on, the bohemian invasion began, pioneered by Edgar Allan Poe, who moved to 85 W3rd Street in 1845. Fellow literary habitués included Mark Twain, O. Henry, Walt Whitman, F. Scott Fitzgerald and Eugene O'Neill. New York University arrived in Washington Square in 1831. Post World War II, bohemia became beatnik; a group of abstract artists, centered around Jackson Pollock, Mark Rothko and Willem de Kooning, also found a home here.

Freedom parades   When police raided the Stonewall Inn on June 28 1969, and arrested gay men for illegally buying drinks, they set off the Stonewall Riots—the birth of the Gay Rights movement. The Inn was on Christopher Street, which became the main drag (no pun intended) of New York's gay community.

Union Square

For proof that New York is always evolving, see Union Square. A "needle park" in the 1970s, it's now where downtown and up meet, with great restaurants, a wild café scene and the city's biggest and best Greenmarket.

Not those Unions Laid out in 1839, Union Square had close encounters with socialism though its name actually refers to the union of Broadway and 4th Avenue. It was a mecca for soapbox orators in the first three decades of the 20th century, then, during the 1930 Depression, 35,000 unemployed rallied here en route to City Hall to demand work; workers' May Day celebrations convened here, too. Later, Andy Warhol picked up the vibes, set up his factory, and began publishing his style mag, *Interview*, where once the *Daily Worker* had been produced.

Green In summer, the park teems with office refugees, sharing the lawn with an equestrian George Washington by John Quincy Adams Ward, an Abe Lincoln by Henry Kirke Brown and a Marquis de Lafayette, which Frédéric-Auguste Bartholdi (of Statue of Liberty fame) gave the city in 1876. Monday, Wednesday, Friday and Saturday are Greenmarket days. An entire culture has grown around this collation of stalls overflowing with homegrown and homemade produce from New England farmers, fishers, bakers and growers. Cult highlights include maple candies, Amish cheeses, the Pretzel Man (and his pretzels), fresh clams and sugarfree muffins.

THE BASICS

➕ D15–E15
✉ W14th–17th streets, Park Avenue South, Broadway
☎ Greenmarket 212/788-7900
🕒 Greenmarket Mon, Wed, Fri, Sat 8–6
🍴 Numerous
🚇 4, 5, 6, L , N, R 14th Street, Union Square
🚌 M3
♿ Poor

HIGHLIGHTS

● Saturday Greenmarket
● Union Square Café
● Jazz at Blue Water Grill
● Amish Farms stall
● Pretzel Man
● Toys R Us and Virgin Megastore
● American Savings Bank building
● Seafood stall
● Apple season

More to See

BLOCK BEAUTIFUL

This picturesque, tree-lined 1920s row really is called this. Also see the pretty square nearby, centered on private Gramercy Park (see opposite page).
🞤 E15 ⊠ E19th Street (Irving Place/Third Avenue) Ⓠ N, R 14th Street Union Square; 6 23rd Street

CHELSEA GALLERIES

The main art district is way west.
● **Andrea Rosen** ⊠ 525 W24th Street ☎ 212/637-6000
● **Chelsea Art Museum** ⊠ 556 W22nd Street ☎ 212/255-0719
● **Dia Center for the Arts** ⊠ 548 W22nd Street ☎ 212/989-5566
● **Gagosian** ⊠ 555 W24th Street ☎ 212/741-1111
● **Greene Naftali** ⊠ 526 W26th Street, 8th floor ☎ 212/463-7770
● **Marianne Boesky** ⊠ 535 W22nd Street ☎ 212/680-9889
● **Mary Boone** ⊠ 541 W24th Street ☎ 212/752-2929
● **Matthew Marks** ⊠ 522 W22nd Street; 523 W24th Street ☎ 212/243-0200
● **Max Protech** ⊠ 511 W22nd Street ☎ 212/633-6999
● **Paula Cooper** ⊠ 534 W21st Street ☎ 212/255-1105
● **Rupert Goldsworthy** ⊠ 453 W17th Street ☎ 212/414-4560
● **Sean Kelly** ⊠ 528 W29th Street ☎ 212/239-1181
● **Sonnabend** ⊠ 536 W22nd Street ☎ 212/627-1018
● **White Box** ⊠ 525 W26th Street ☎ 212/714-2347
● **White Columns** ⊠ 320 W13th Street ☎ 212/924-4212

FLATIRON BUILDING

This 1902 skyscraper was named after its amazing shape: an isosceles triangle with a sharp angle pointing uptown. This instantly recognizable and memorable landmark was designed by Daniel Burnham in 1902.
🞤 E14 ⊠ 175 5th Avenue (E22nd/23rd streets) Ⓠ N, R 23rd Street

GRACE CHURCH

An outstanding James Renwick-designed Gothic Revival church of

The iconic Flatiron Building

Detail of the interior of Grace Church

the first half of the 19th century. The stained glass is superb, as is the mosaic floor. The original steeple, constructed in wood was replaced by a marble one in 1888.

🕂 E16 ✉ 100 Broadway ☎ 212/254-2000 🕓 Mon–Fri 10–4, Sun services 🚇 N, R, W, 6

GRAMERCY PARK

Peaceful and pleasant to stroll, Gramercy is centered on the epony-mous park. The park itself is private and remains locked to all but the residents of the surrounding square. The elegant National Arts Club (15 Gramercy Park South/20th Street, tel 212/475-3424) has frequent events open to non-members.

🕂 E15 🚇 N, R, 6 23rd Street

THE MEATPACKING DISTRICT

Bordered roughly by Jane and W13th Streets and 9th Avenue/Greenwich Street, this district was named for its wholesale meat warehouses. Then, around the millennium the area got so hip so fast, it quickly became not hip

at all. But its tangle of boutiques, bars, clubs and restaurants is still something of a magnet for young New Yorkers.

🕂 Off map at C16 🚇 A, C, E, L 14th Street

ST. MARKS IN THE BOWERY

The church was built on the site of Peter Stuyvesant's chapel on his farm (*bouwerie*). His grandson sold parcels of the land in today's East Village, and the church purchased the site for the nominal fee of a dollar. Stuyvesant and many of his descendants are buried in the churchyard.

🕂 F16 ✉ E10th Street ☎ 212/674-6377 🕓 Events only 🚇 F, V

WASHINGTON SQUARE: "THE ROW" AND ARCH

"The Row" (1–13 north side) housed movers and shakers of 19th-century New York City—read Henry James' *Washington Square*. At the heart of the park is the Arch, designed by Stanford White where you can watch New Yorkers enjoying themselves.

🕂 D17 🚇 N, R 8th Street; A, C, E, B, D, F, Q W4th Street

Entertainment in Washington Square Greenwich Village

Metropolitan Life Insurance Building

Greenwich Village

Greenwich and West Village from then till now.

DISTANCE: 1.5 miles (2.5km) **ALLOW:** 35 minutes

START

WASHINGTON SQUARE
🚇 A, B, C, D, F, V W4th Street

1 Start in Washington Square Park and walk under the Arch, three blocks north along 5th Avenue. Turn left into W10th Street until you reach the Avenue of the Americas.

2 Cross the avenue and continue on W10th, passing the ornate Jefferson Market Library built in 1877. Ahead is 4 Patchin Place, the home of the poet e e cummings.

3 Turn left onto Greenwich Avenue and continue until you reach the junction with Christopher Street where you turn right and pass many cute homewares boutiques.

4 Stop on Christopher Park and say hello to the realistic quartet of bronze people on a bench by George Segal commemorating the gay rights riots nearby.

END

AVENUE OF THE AMERICAS
🚇 A, C 14th Street

8 To reach the subway go north on Washington again and turn right on W14th to the A, C, E, L on the corner of 8th Avenue.

7 Walk until you see the Hudson River across West Side Highway. Continue north three blocks up West Street and turn right on Bethune. At Washington turn left and in four blocks you'll be in the Meatpacking District. Explore the cobbled streets.

6 Continue on Bleecker for four blocks. Just before W11th Street, stop for cupcakes at the Magnolia Bakery then turn left on 11th, walk two blocks and go left on Greenwich Street, taking the next right on Perry.

5 Exit the park on Christopher Street, cross 7th Avenue, continue for one block, turn right on Bleecker Street.

ABC CARPET AND HOME

Here are seven floors of meticulously edited homewares, from four-poster beds to handkerchiefs, which share an esthetic that mixes Victorian brothel, mid-19th-century design museum, Venetian palace and deluxe hotel. Don't let the bazaar atmosphere fool you into expecting bargains.
➕ E15 ✉ 888 Broadway/19th Street ☎ 212/473-3000 Ⓜ 4, 5, 6, N, Q, R, W 14th Street/Union Street

CHELSEA MARKET

More than a store, this enormous city-block-size building is several villages' worth of food boutiques, bakeries, cafés, coffee shops and delis under one roof. Even if you're not hungry, stroll through for the architect-honed industrial warehouse meets ancient cave atmosphere.
➕ C15 ✉ 75 9th Avenue/15th Street ☎ 212/243-6005 Ⓜ A, C, E, L 14th Street

DSW AND FILENE'S

That's "Designer Shoe Warehouse" with Prada, Kate Spade, Via Spiga et al. represented. Upstairs is a three-story Filene's where Dolce & Gabanna, Alberta Feretti and Stella McCartney are among the labels with regular off-price off-season items.
➕ E15 ✉ 4 Union Square South (University Place)

☎ 212/674-2146 Ⓜ L, N, Q, R, W, \$, 5, 6 Union Square

GREENMARKET

Farmers travel from the tri-state area to this outdoor farmers' market that has rejuvenated the entire Union Square area.
➕ D15–E15 Ⓜ 4, 5, 6, N, R, L Union Square

JEFFREY NEW YORK

The coolest thing in the Meatpacking District is this compact department store of fashion so high it has vertigo. A resident DJ, a spacious all-white interior, a small but trendy cosmetics department and nonpushy assistants make for a pleasant visit—and an expensive one if you fall for the wares.
➕ Off map at C15 ✉ 449 W14th Street/Washington Street ☎ 212/206-1272 Ⓜ A, C, E, L 14th Street

KATE'S PAPERIE

The beautiful handmade stationery is overwhelming at this SoHo boutique.
➕ E18 ✉ 561 Broadway ☎ 212/941-9816 Ⓜ N, R Prince Street

JEFFREY LOEHMANN'S

The Manhattan branch of a Brooklyn institution, this five-floor fashion emporium is best for its Back Room, where designers—Donna Karan, Calvin Klein, even Valentino—lurk, at small prices.
➕ C15 ✉ 101 Seventh Avenue (17th Street) ☎ 212/352-0856 Ⓜ 1, 9 18th Street

MARC JACOBS

Fashion's favorite darling put once-Bohemian Bleecker Street on the map.
➕ C16 ✉ 1385, 403, 405 Bleecker Street ☎ 212/924-0026 Ⓜ 1, 2 Christopher Sreet/Sheridan Square

PAUL SMITH

Magnificent, expensive menswear for the fashion conscious gentleman.
➕ E15 ✉ 108 5th Avenue (16th Street) ☎ 212/627-9770 Ⓜ 4, 5, 6, N, R, L Union Street

SCOOP

Hip labels from Daryl K to Tocca and Katayone Adeli, plus cult items like James Perse T's.
➕ E18 ✉ 532 Broadway (Spring Street) ☎ 212/925-2886 Ⓜ F, S Broadway Lafayette; N, R Prince Street

Entertainment and Nightlife

APT

Part club, part music venue, part apartment, this hidden (no sign) swanky lounge hosts some wild nights.
⊞ Off map at C16 ✉ 419 W13th Street (9th/10th avenues) ☎ 212/414-4245 Ⓢ A, C 14th Street

DUPLEX

Drag queens and downtown crooners sit around the piano bar and have a great time.
⊞ D16 ✉ 61 Christopher Street (7th Avenue) ☎ 212/255-5438 Ⓢ 1, 9 Christopher Street

GOTHAM COMEDY CLUB

Venue for up-and-coming comedians.
⊞ C14 ✉ 208 W23rd Street (7th/8th Avenues) ☎ 212/367-9000 Ⓢ N, R 23rd Street; F, Path 23rd Street

IRVING PLAZA

You never know who might show up on the calendar for this medium-size venue.
⊞ E15 ✉ 17 Irving Place ☎ 212/777-6800 Ⓢ N, R, 4, 6 Union Square

JOE'S PUB

The red velvet bar and petite performance space named after Joseph Papp, founder of the theater that houses it, has an always-interesting line-up of torch singers, comedians, magicians, new wave burlesque artistes and more.
⊞ F16 ✉ The Public Theater, 425 Lafayette Street/ Astor Place ☎ 212/539-8777 Ⓢ N, R, W 8th Street/6 Astor Place

MERCER HOTEL LOBBY BAR

The friendly service at this tiny Soho hotspot makes for a pleasant, chic experience.
⊞ E18 ✉ 147 Mercer Street (Prince Street) ☎ 212/966-6060 Ⓢ N Prince Street

MERCURY LOUNGE

A laid-back atmosphere that suits eclectic performers. Very few seats.
⊞ F17 ✉ 217 East Houston Street ☎ 212/260-4700 Ⓢ F 2nd Avenue

O BAR

The bar of Ono, the Japanese restaurant in the Gansevoort Hotel which functions as an anchor for Meatpacking madness, is as gorgeous to look at as its patrons, but better than the gold-walled interior is the terrace garden—a mob scene on a not-too-sweaty summer Thursday night.
⊞ C15 ✉ 18 9th Avenue/ 13th Street ☎ 212/660-6766 Ⓢ A, C, E, L 14th Street

PERFORMING GARAGE

The home of the avant garde productions of the Wooster Group, led by Elizabeth LeCompte and often featuring her husband, Willem Dafoe.
⊞ E18 ✉ 33 Wooster Street (Broome/Grand streets) ☎ 212/966-3651 Ⓢ A, C, E, J, M, N, Q, R, W, Z, 1, 9, 6 Canal Street

PETE'S TAVERN

This 1864 Gramercy Park Victorian saloon is where O. Henry wrote *The Gift of the Magi*. No matter how hokey its history, it remains a favorite, thanks to brick walls, dim light and a welcoming ambiance.
⊞ E15 ✉ 129 E18th Street ☎ 212/473-7676 Ⓢ N, R, 4, 6 Union Street

PS 122

A converted public school that hosts a range of acts from the bizarre to the poignant.
⊞ F16 ✉ First Avenue (9th Street) ☎ 212/477-5288 Ⓢ N, R 8th Street, F 2nd Avenue

CABARET

The term has undergone so many image-overhauls, it's now settled into being a catch-all for entertainment options ranging from women-only male burlesque shows (Show, 135 W41st Street, 212/675-0988) to drag queen lip-synching and, in the case of Lips (2 Bank Street, 212/675-7710), Bitchy Bingo. Joe's Pub (left) is among the venues that often offer what you might call classic, though modernized, cabaret.

Restaurants

PRICES

Prices are approximate, based on a 3-course meal for one person.

$$$	over $60
$$	$40–$60
$	under $40

BETTE ($$)

Nightlife queen (Bungalow 8, Lot 61) Amy Sacco added restaurateur to her job description when she opened this place in late 2005. With carpet and art deco chandeliers on the ceiling, it feels homey—which isn't so surprising since it's named after her mom and Sacco lives in one of the London Terrace apartments upstairs. The food is comfy, too: chicken-liver dumplings; lobster ravioli; strip steak with truffled fries and an amazing Valrhona chocolate pudding.
✚ Off map at C14 ✉ 461 W23rd Street/9th–10th Avenues ☎ 212/366-0404 🚇 A, C, E 23rd Street

DEL POSTO ($$$)

Mario Batali is New York's rotundly ebullient TV-friendly patron saint of interesting Italian food, known for rustic dishes and casual ambience. In his early-2006 latest, though, he changed the rules: this is a swanky, deco-looking, grown-up, big-night-out grand restaurant, with piano

player, theatrical tableside preparations and what may be NYC's only valet parking. Of course, it works beautifully.
✚ Off map at C15 ✉ 85 10th Avenue/ 16th Street ☎ 212/497-8090 🚇 A, C, E, L 14th Street

GOTHAM BAR AND GRILL ($$$)

This restaurant epitomizes New York grandeur. World-class dishes like rack of lamb with swiss chard and roasted shallots have delighted New Yorkers since 1984. The soaring space is light and airy with modern chandeliers.
✚ E16 ✉ 12 E12th Street ☎ 212/620-4020 🕐 Closed Sat, Sun lunch 🚇 N, R, 4, 6 Union Square

GRAMERCY TAVERN ($$–$$$)

As food temples go, Gramercy is laid-back,

GIANT SUSHI

For the sushi connoisseur, Yama ($–$$) may not offer the best there is, but it does serve the biggest sushi and it is very good. Sadly, many people share this view, and the tiny place is engulfed with salivating sushi wolves, lining up for hours.
✚ E15 ✉ 49 Irving Place (17th Street) ☎ 212/475-0969 🕐 Closed Sun 🚇 N, R, 4, 5, 6 14th Street (Union Square)

especially if you eat in the less expensive no-reservations area in front, where the food is more rustic. Tom Colicchio uses only the freshest market produce in his hearty, utterly reliable new-American food.
✚ E15 ✉ 42 E20th Street (Broadway/Park Avenue) ☎ 212/477-0777 🚇 6, N, R 23rd Street

THE RED CAT ($–$$)

Jimmy Bradley's red-painted, laid-back restaurant is ideal for dinner after a gallery visit in West Chelsea. It's all a bit Southern Italy (sweet pea risotto cake).
✚ Off map at C14 ✉ 227 10th Avenue (23rd/24th streets) ☎ 212/ 242-1122 🚇 C, E 23rd Street

THE SPOTTED PIG ($$)

It's an Anglo-style gastro-pub, so popular it doubled in size, then it was awarded a Michelin star in the first NY guide, lo, you have to wait an hour or two for a table (you can't reserve). Minimize the pain by coming at off-hours, and order the gnudia kind of ricotta-spinach gnocchi that chef April Bloomfield has made her own.
✚ C16 ✉ 314 West 11th Street/Greenwich Street ☎ 212/620-0393 🚇 A, B, C, D, F, Q, V, W4th Street

Definitely a must for visitors to Manhattan, this district has leading museums, a revitalized Times Square, Grand Central Terminal plus the magnet for shoppers—Fifth Avenue with its legendary emporiums.

8

West 59th Street

9

COLUMBUS CIRCLE

59th Street Columbus Circle

Central Park South

West 58th Street

West 58th Street

East 59th Street

East 58th Street

57th Street

57th Street

Carnegie Hall

WEST 57TH STREET

WEST 57TH STREET

EAST 57TH STREET

West 56th Street

Trump Tower

Dahes Museum of Art

West 55th Street

West 55th Street

East 55th Street

BROADWAY

West 54th Street

7th Avenue

West 54th Street

Museum of Modern Art

5th Avenue

West 53rd Street

7th Avenue

West 53rd Street

East 53rd Street

Museum of Arts and Design

Museum of Television and Radio

West 52nd Street

West 52nd Street

East 52nd Street

10

West 51st Street

West 51st Street

St Patrick's Cathedral

Munici Art Soci

Radio City Music Hall

West 50th Street

East 50th Street

50th Street

50th Street

49th Street

47th - 50th Streets Rockefeller Center

West 50th Street

Rockefeller Plaza

G.E. Building

MIDTOWN

West 49th Street

East 49th Street

West 49th Street

Rockefeller Center

West 48th Street

MANHATTA

West 48th Street

East 48th Street

DIAMOND DISTRICT

West 47th Street

West 47th Street

East 47th Street

West 46th Street

West 46th Street

Fifth Avenue

West 45th Street

West 45th Street

East 45th Street

11

West 44th Street

8th Avenue

Times Square

West 44th Street

5th Avenue

East 44th Street

Madison Avenue

International Center of Photography

West 43rd Street

West 43rd Street

East 43rd Street

Holy Cross Church

Reuters Building

42nd Street

5th Avenue

WEST 42ND STREET

WEST 42ND STREET

EAST 42ND STR

9th Avenue

42nd Street Port Authority Bus Terminal

West 41st Street

New Amsterdam Theater

Times Square 42nd Street

Bryant Park

New York Public Library

East 41st Street

DYER AVENUE

West 40th Street

FASHION

West 40th Street

West 39th Street

BROADWAY

West 39th Street

Avenue of the Americas (6th Avenue)

East 39th Street

8th Avenue

West 38th Street

West 38th Street

5th Avenue

East 38th Street

12

West 37th Street

AVENUE

West 37th Street

East 37th Street

Morgan Library

West 36th Street

West 36th Street

East 36th Street

West 35th Street

West 35th Street

East 35th Street

Macy's

West 34th Street

WEST 34TH STREET

EAST 34T

34th Street Penn Station

34th Street Penn Station

34th Street Herald Square

Empire State Building

West 33rd Street

West 33rd Street

East 33rd Street

Madison Square Garden

Pennsylvania Station

West 32nd Street

East 32nd Street

West 31st Street

West 31st Street

East 31st Stre

13

West 30th Street

West 30th Street

East 30th Stre

C

D

Chrysler Building

HIGHLIGHTS

- Spire
- Ceiling mural
- Elevator cabs
- Fourth setback gargoyles
- African marble lobby

TIP

- From here Grand Central Terminal is no distance at all. Head to the Food Court or Oyster Bar for lunch.

"Which is your favorite New York building?" goes the annoying yet perennial question. Nine out of ten people who express a preference pick the Chrysler Building. This should surprise nobody who gazes on it.

King for a year The tower, commissioned from William Van Alen by Walter Chrysler (who asked for something "taller than the Eiffel Tower"), won the world's tallest building competition in 1930—until the Empire State Building went up the next year. Van Alen had been almost beaten by Craig Severance's Bank of Manhattan tower at 40 Wall Street, when his rival, aware of the unofficial race, slung on an extra two feet. Unknown to Severance, though, Van Alen was constructing a 123ft (37m) stainless-steel spire, which he

The Chrysler Building viewed from the Empire State Building (left); the gleaming lobby of the Chrysler Building (middle); detail of the Chrysler Building's stainless steel spire (below)

"slotted" out through the 925 ft (282 m) roof, beating the 927-footer hands down. It is sort of ironic that the best view of the art-deco beauty's top is from the observatory at the Empire State.

Multistory car Every detail of the 77-story build-ing evokes a 1929 Chrysler Plymouth, to be exact. The winged steel gargoyles are modeled on its radiator caps; the building's stepped setbacks carry stylized hubcaps and the entire spire resembles a radiator grill; and this ain't no Toyota. The golden age of cars is further evoked by the stunning lobby, which you can visit to see the art deco detailing in the red marble, granite and chrome interior, surmounted by the 97ft by 100ft (30m by 31m) mural depicting industrial scenes and celebrating "transportation." Don't miss the mar-quetry elevator doors.

THE BASICS

🔖 E11

✉ 405 Lexington Avenue (42nd Street)

🕐 Mon–Fri 7am–6pm; closed holidays

🚇 4, 5, 6, 7, S 42nd Street, Grand Central

🚌 M101, M102

🚉 Metro North, Grand Central

♿ Good

🎟 Free

Empire State Building TOP 25

HIGHLIGHTS

● The view: by day, at dusk and by night
● The view up from 34th Street
● TowerCams
● Observatory Audio Tour
● Lights on the top stories

TIP

● The colored lights at the summit were introduced in 1976 and are changed to mark different events. You can avoid the line (though not the security one) by printing out advance tickets from the website.

It was not Fay Wray's fault, nor Cary Grant's in *An Affair to Remember*, that this is the most famous skyscraper in the world. Rather, its fame is the reason it has appeared in every New York movie. You have to climb this.

King for 40 years This is the very definition of "skyscraper," and it was the highest man-made thing until the late, lamented World Trade Center was built in the 1970s. Now it is once again the tallest building in New York. Construction began in 1929, not long before the great Wall Street Crash, and by the time it was topped out in 1931—construction went at the superfast rate of four stories a week—so few could afford to rent space, they called it "the Empty State Building." Only the popularity of its observatories kept the wolves from the

The Empire State Building (left and below); the buildings of Midtown look small when viewed from the Empire State Building (middle top); the lobby (middle left); the observation deck (middle right)

door. These viewpoints still attract 35,000 visitors a day. The 86th floor Observatory, with its glass-enclosed, climate-controlled area, is a highlight, but if you can't make the trip, the live online ESB TowerCams provide a live video feed of the view from the very top.

Facts It is 1,250ft (381m) high, with 102 floors. The frame contains 60,000 tons of steel, 10 million bricks line the building, and there are 6,500 windows. The speediest of the 73 elevators climb 1,200ft (355m) per minute. The speediest runners in the annual Empire State Run-Up climb almost 170 steps per minute, making the 1,860 steps to the 102nd floor in 11 minutes—though normal people take about half an hour to climb down! After endless waits and crushes, management has closed the 102nd floor to the public.

THE BASICS

www.esbnyc.com
🚏 D13
✉ 350 5th Avenue (W34th Street)
☎ 212/736-3100
🕐 Daily 9.30am–midnight; last admission 11.15pm
🍴 Snack bar
Ⓜ B, D, F, N, Q, R, V, W34th Street
🚌 M1, M2, M3, M4, M5, M16, M34
🚆 PATH 33rd Street
♿ Good
💲 Moderate

Fifth Avenue

HIGHLIGHTS

- Shopping!
- Empire State Building
- Rockefeller Center
- The Met
- The Guggenheim
- The Cooper-Hewitt

TIP

- Try to see a parade—
St. Patrick's Day Parade, the
biggest, is on March 17.

Think of shopping in New York and Fifth Avenue is likely to be your next thought. But there is more here: Museums, smart hotels, private clubs and landmark buildings rub shoulders with FAO Schwartz, Tiffany's, Cartier and Saks Fifth Avenue.

Tradition and invention Fifth Avenue runs all the way from Washington Square Park up past Central Park and it houses some of the most pricey and notable real estate in New York. Walk along the avenue and you'll pass the Flatiron Building (▷ 42), Empire State Building (▷ 54), the New York Public Library (▷ 61), the Rockefeller Center (▷ 62), the Metropolitan Museum of Art (▷ 80), the Guggenheim (▷ 78), St. Patrick's Cathedral (▷ 66) and the Cooper-Hewitt (▷ 76). These are just a few of the buildings that repre-

Fifth Avenue on the street (left) and up in the air during a parade (below)

sent the development of Fifth Avenue from a
sought-after address lined with mansions of the
wealthy to important artery of this vibrant city.

Shop, shop, shop The shopping venues of favor
with kids will be the reinvented FAO Schwartz and
the Disney Store. Parents might prefer the jewelry
emporia of Tiffany & Co. and Cartier, and the
famous department stores. Saks Fifth Avenue has
been at its Renaissance-style building (between
50th and 51st streets) since 1922. The poshest
store of all, Bergdorf Goodman is at 57th Street
and fashion mecca; Henri Bendel is at 56th.

Relax Two excellent hotels stand on 55th Street,
the Peninsula New York, with great vistas from its
Pentop Bar and Terrace Grill and the St-Regis
Hotel with the King Cole Bar.

THE BASICS

✚ E12–E9
✉ From Washington
Square to the Harlem River
🚇 4, 5, 6
🚌 M1, M2, M3, M4

57

HIGHLIGHTS

- Main Concourse ceiling
- Oyster Bar
- The Food Court
- Mercury on the 42nd Street facade
- The clock
- The 75-ft (23-m) arched windows
- Grand Staircase

TIP

- Immortalize yourself at the StoryBooth in The Biltmore Room next to tracks 41 and 42: it's the flagship of the remarkable oral history project (www.storycorps.net).

Don't call it a station. All tracks terminate here, which makes this—yes—a terminal. The Beaux-Arts building bustles like no place else. As the saying goes— stand here long enough and the entire world passes by.

Heart of the nation "Grand Central Station!" bellowed (erroneously) the 1937 opening of the eponymous NBC radio drama; "Beneath the glitter and swank of Park Avenue…Crossroads of a million private lives!…Heart of the nation's greatest city…" And so it is, and has been since 1871 when the first, undersized version was opened by Commodore Cornelius Vanderbilt, who had bought up all the city's railroads, just like on a giant Monopoly board. See him in bronze below Jules-Alexis Coutans' allegorical statuary on the

The busy main concourse at Grand Central Terminal (left); the entrance to the terminal (below); detail of the clock (bottom left); people riding the escalator (bottom right)

main facade (south, 42nd Street). The current building dates from 1913 and is another Beaux-Arts glory, its design modeled partly on the Paris Opéra by architects Warren and Wetmore. William Wilgus was the logician responsible for traffic-marshaling, while Reed & Stem were the overall engineers. Look up at the main concourse ceiling for the stunning sight of 2,500 "stars" in a cerulean sky, with medieval-style zodiac signs by French artist Paul Helleu.

Look within The fame of the four-faced clock atop the information booth is out of proportion to its size. Below ground, is a warren of 32 miles (52km) of tracks, tunnels and vaulted chambers, in one the famed Oyster Bar resides. The Food Court is virtually a new neighborhood. Be careful what you say here—the acoustics are amazing.

THE BASICS

www.
grandcentralterminal.com
✚ E11
✉ Park Avenue (42nd Street)
☎ 212/532-4900; Story Booth 800/850-4406
🕐 Daily 5.30am–1.30am; Story Booth daily 24 hours
🍴 Restaurant, café/bar, snack bars
Ⓢ 4, 5, 6, 7, S 42nd Street, Grand Central
🚌 M101, 102 Grand Central
🚆 Metro North, Grand Central
♿ Good 🎟 Free
❓ Tours Wed 12.30pm. Meet by information booth in Main Concourse

Museum of Modern Art

Views of MoMa (far left and left); David and Peggy Rockefeller Building (below)

THE BASICS

www.moma.org
✚ D10
✉ 11 W53rd Street
☎ 212/708–9400
🕐 Sat–Mon, Wed, Thu 10.30–5.30, Fri 10.30–8
🍴 Restaurant
Ⓔ E, V 5th Avenue/53rd Street; B, D, F 47th–50th Street
🚌 M1, 2, 3, 4, 5
💰 Expensive; free Fri 4–8

HIGHLIGHTS

● *Water Lilies*, Monet (1920)
● *Dance*, Matisse (1909)
● *Les Demoiselles d'Avignon*, Picasso (1907)
● *Starry Night*, Van Gogh (1889)
● *Broadway Boogie-Woogie*, Mondrian (1942–43)
● *One*, Pollock (1950)
● *Flag*, Jasper Johns (1954–55)

Opened in November 2004, the new MOMA building, designed by Japanese architect Yoshio Taniguchi, has been called a work of art, and at 630,000sq ft (58,527sq m) it has nearly twice the capacity of the old museum.

Van Gogh to Man Ray Founded on the 1931 bequest of Lillie P. Bliss, which consisted of 235 works, the collections now amount to about 100,000 pieces. These include household objects, photography, graphic design, conceptual art and industrial design.

Postimpressionists to graffiti artists The collection starts in the late 19th century, with the Postimpressionists and Fauvists. Among the 20th-century movements represented are Cubism, Futurism, Expressionism, Surrealism, Abstract Expressionism, Pop (Oldenburg, Dine, Rauschenberg and Warhol) and the "Graffiti" work of Keith Haring and Jean-Michel Basquiat.

Even more modern A sunlighted 110ft (33m) high atrium affording a view of the beloved Abby Aldrich Rockefeller Sculpture Garden heralds the all-new MOMA, featuring much use of glass, granite, aluminum and floods of light. Taniguchi designed individual galleries specifically for the media they house, including new ones for contemporary art and new media. A restaurant operated by restaurateur Danny Meyer raises the glamour quotient, that is, if this modern art collection didn't already do so.

A nearly full Reading Room (below); sign on the outside of the building (right)

NY Public Library

QUIET ZONE

Why are we sending you to a library on your vacation? Because the New York Public Library's Central Research Building is a great, white, hushed palace, beautiful to behold even if you have no time to open a book.

The building Carrère and Hastings (who also designed the Frick, ▷ 77) were the architects of what is generally thought the city's best representative of the Beaux-Arts style—the sumptuous yet classical French school that flourished in 1880–1920 in New York. A pair of lions, which Mayor La Guardia christened Patience and Fortitude, flank the majestic stair that leads directly into the vaulted, carved white marble temple of Astor Hall. The lions are themselves flanked by fountains, "Truth" and "Beauty." Behind this briefly stood New York's version of London's Crystal Palace, built for the first American World's Fair in 1853. Like the London one, it burned down. Inside, see temporary exhibitions in the Gottesman Hall, and look up! The carved oak ceiling is sublime; read in the two-block-long Main Reading Room; see library collection rarities in the Salomon Room; and don't miss the Richard Haas murals of NYC publishing houses in the De Witt Wallace Periodical Room.

The books The library owns more than 15 million books, most living in the 82 branches. This building is dedicated to research. The CATNYP computer can disgorge any of the 16 million manuscripts or 3 million books from the 92 miles (148km) of stacks in 10 minutes flat.

THE BASICS

www.nypl.org

⊞ D11

✉ 476 5th Avenue (42nd Street)

☎ 212/930-0800

🕐 Tue–Wed 11–7.30, Thu–Sat 10–6; closed holidays

🍴 Kiosks outside (not winter)

🚇 4, 5, 6, 7, S 42nd Street Grand Central

🚌 M101, M102

🚆 Metro North, Grand Central

♿ Good

💵 Free

HIGHLIGHTS

● Patience and Fortitude
● "Truth" and "Beauty"
● T. S. Eliot's typescript of *The Waste Land*
● Jefferson's handwritten Declaration of Independence
● Astor Hall
● Thomas Hastings' flagpost bases
● Gottesman Hall ceiling

MIDTOWN

TOP 25

61

Rockefeller Center

People (left) and a statue (middle) outside the center; ice-skating at Christmas (below)

HIGHLIGHTS

- GE Building, outside
- GE Building's lobbies
- NBC Studio tour
- Skating in winter
- Sea Grill restaurant
- Radio City Music Hall
- Channel Gardens
- Prometheus (1934)
- Atlas (5th Avenue, 50th–51st streets)

This small village of famous art deco buildings provides many of those "Gee, this is New York" moments: especially in winter when you see ice-skaters ringed by the flags of the UN and gaze up at the massive tree.

Prometheus is here The buildings' bible, Willensky and White's *AIA Guide to NYC*, calls the 19-building Rockefeller Center "The greatest urban complex of the 20th century." So the architectural importance of the center—especially the elongated ziggurat GE Building (better known as the RCA Building)—is beyond dispute, but it's still easy to enjoy the place. Rest on a Channel Gardens bench, enjoy the seasonal foliage and gaze on the lower plaza, the rink and Paul Manship's "Prometheus."

Rockefeller the Younger The realization of John D. Rockefeller Jr.'s grand scheme to outdo dad (Mister Standard Oil) provided work for a quarter of a million souls during the Depression. In 1957, Marilyn Monroe detonated the dynamite for the Time & Life building's foundations, and the Center was still growing into the 1970s.

Conan and Rockettes For many years, the NBC Studios in the GE Building hosted the hip TV talk show *Late Night with David Letterman*. Dave decamped to CBS, and the now-famous Conan O'Brien was plucked from obscurity to host the spot. Over on Avenue of the Americas is Radio City Music Hall, landmark home to the Rockettes.

Stretch limo in Times Square (below); looking up from Times Square (right)

Times Square

"The Crossroads of the World," one-time symbol of Manhattan glitz and glam, is an area New Yorkers love to hate—especially since it is sanitized. You may disagree as you explore the big stores and get dazzled by the neon.

Longacre The junction of Broadway and 7th Avenue wasn't even called Times Square until 1904. It was "The Longacre" until Times Tower, the new home of the *New York Times*, was finished. Almost immediately, the invention of neon light, the opening of the first subway line and the decision to site the city's New Year celebration here conspired to make the triangular square the de facto center of Manhattan.

On Broadway The theaters moved in and Broadway, the Great White Way, became synonymous with bigtime showbiz: popular theatrical—especially musical—division. By 1914 there were 43 theaters in the immediate vicinity; after multiple closings, refurbishments and reopenings, there are 22 of them today.

Best of Times, Worst of Times By the 1970s Times Square was one of the most crime-ridden neighborhoods in the city, rife with porn emporia of all kinds, drug-dealing and assorted vileness. The dawn of the 1990s saw the rebirth with several city-run and independent organizations working to clean up and re-glamorize. As the giant stores, state-of-the-art illuminations and even the Armed Forces recruiting Station show, it worked.

THE BASICS

🚌 C11–D11
ℹ️ Times Square Visitors Center ✉️ 1560 Broadway
☎️ 212/768-1560
🚇 1, 2, 3, 7, N, Q, R, S, W Times Square
🕐 8am–8pm
❓ Free "Times Square Exposé" tour, Friday at noon, rain or shine

HIGHLIGHTS

- New Victory Theater
- Shubert Alley
- Toys R Us indoor Ferris wheel
- ABC's *Good Morning* studio: 44th/Broadway
- Live appearances at MTC TRL studio
- New Year's Eve ball drop

TIP

- The cash-only TKTS booth at 47th Street and Broadway is good for same-day theater tickets for 20–50 percent off. It's open daily 3–8pm for evening shows; Wednesday and Saturday 10–2, Sunday 11–3 for matinees.

MIDTOWN ★ **TOP 25**

Shopping Spree

A restrained display window (left); shoppers thronging Fifth Avenue (below)

THE BASICS

Soho Crawl
🚇 N, R Prince Street

Madison Avenue
🚇 Lexington Avenue-63rd Street

HIGHLIGHTS

● Areas not covered here include (but are not restricted to) Herald Square (Macy's and huge branches of H&M, Old Navy, Gap, Victoria's Secret); Fifth Avenue (▷ 56); the *other* Fifth Avenue in Park Slope, plus other Brooklyn strips at Smith Street (Boerum Hill/ Carroll Gardens) and Bedford Avenue (Williamsburg) all teeming with enchanting independent boutiques. Then there's Nolita, the grid of dinky high-fashion store centered on Elizabeth Street; the multiple hipster emporia of the Lower East Side and the "big box" stores of Chelsea.

What is great about shopping in New York is the way you come across cool stores all over the place, and also the sheer quantity of shopping neighborhoods. Here is an easy two-part shopping mission that you can manage (just about) in one day.

Soho crawl Start with a coffee and pastry at Dean and Deluca (Broadway/Prince). You're opposite the museumlike Prada store with Kate's Paperie (▷ 45) just down the block. Huge H&M and Zara stores are also here. Head south down Broadway for Scoop (▷ 45) and branches of the underwear queen, Victoria's Secret (at Spring) and the cosmetics sweet shop Sephora (555 Broadway); Banana Republic (women at 552, men at 494) and Old Navy; you'll also see shoe stores carrying sneakers and casual brands like Frye, Dansko and Merrill (for fabulous fashion shoes go one block east to Otto Tootsi Plohound at 273 Lafayette Street). On the east side of the street is the downtown branch of Bloomingdales (504 Broadway). Now head down Broome, stopping at Gourmet Garage (▷ 32) for a snack and checking out Kate Spade accessories opposite and head north on Mercer, Greene or Wooster. Here you're on your own lots of stores to explore.

Madison Avenue The next leg is easier. Take the F from Broadway Lafayette to Lexington Avenue/ 63rd Street, walk west across Park Avenue to Madison Avenue and hang a left. Head straight to Barneys (▷ 85), then work your way slowly down. Well done!

INTERNATIONAL CENTER OF PHOTOGRAPHY

In the heart of Midtown, the ICP is both a school and a museum. Temporary exhibitions are always on view, and the permanent collection has 60,000 photographs ranging from old daguerreotypes to iris prints, mainly from American and European reportage and documentation from the 1930s to the present. There are photographs by such well-known names as Henri Cartier-Bresson, Elliott Erwitt and Harold Edgerton, along with an impressive collection of 13,000 original prints by Weegee, who photographed crime scenes and New York nightlife in the 1930s and 1940s.

🔢 D11 ✉ 1133 Avenue of the Americas ☎ 212/857-0000 🕐 Tue–Thu 10–5, Fri 10–8, Sat–Sun 10–7 🚇 B, D, F, V

"LIPSTICK BUILDING"

This likeable 1986 show-off is by John Burgee with Philip Johnson.

🔢 F10 ✉ 885 3rd Avenue (55th/56th streets) 🚇 6 51st Street

MADISON SQUARE GARDEN

Above Penn Station, this popular venue is for concerts and major sports events. It is also the home of the New York Knicks basketball team

🔢 C13 ✉ 4 Penn Plaza ☎ 212/465-6741 🚇 A,C, E, 1, 2, 3, 9 34th Street/Penn Station

MORGAN LIBRARY

Reopened in late April 2006, the library's Renzo Piano extension has doubled its gallery space and added a new Reading Room and Madison Avenue entrance. The collection was started by John Pierpont Morgan, a wealthy financier, at the end of the 19th century. The collection includes the 9th-century Lindau Gospels, a rare vellum copy of the Gutenberg Bible, the medieval Dutch masterpiece *The Hours of Catherine of Cleves*, scores by such composers as Beethoven, Mozart and Puccini and manuscripts by authors Jane Austen, Charles Dickens, Henry David Thoreau and Mark Twain.

🔢 E12 ✉ 29 East 36th Street ☎ 212/590-0300 🕐 Not available when writing 🚇 6

MIDTOWN

★

MORE TO SEE

Inside the Morgan Library

MUSEUM OF TELEVISION AND RADIO

The museum was established in 1989 on land donated by William S. Paley, a former chairman of broadcasting giant CBS. The archive of 100,000 tapes of programs, and commercials span 75 years. When you arrive, make a reservation to use the computer catalog on the fourth floor to locate what interests you, then reserve it and watch it in one of the museum's consoles. Or you can take in a show or two at one of the screening rooms or theaters. Seminars and classes, as well as exhibitions, are held throughout the year.

➕ D10 ✉ 25 West 52nd Street
☎ 212/621-6800 🕐 Tue–Sun noon–6, Thu until 8, Fri theater programs 🚇 E, V

ST. PATRICK'S CATHEDRAL

James Renwick's Gothic Revival cathedral is the US's biggest for Roman Catholics, seating around 2,200. It is popular with visitors too and annually receives 3 million of them.

➕ E10 ✉ 5th Avenue (50th Street)

☎ 212/753-2261 🕐 6am–9pm 🚇 6 51st Street; E, F 5th Avenue

TRUMP TOWER

"Glitz" captured in pink marble and glass. The top floors are made up of apartments, while below is a six-floor atrium with shops, waterfalls and greenery.

➕ E9 ✉ 725 Fifth Avenue at 56th Street
☎ 212/832-2000 🕐 8am–10pm
🍴 Several 🚇 E, F 5th Avenue

UNITED NATIONS HEADQUARTERS

The 544ft (166m) Secretariat building that dominates the site opened in 1950. Alongside are the General Assembly building, the Conference building (fronting the river) and the Dag Hammarskjöld Library. A 45-minute guided tour covers the General Assembly Hall and Security Council Chamber.

➕ G11 ✉ 1st Avenue at 45th Street
☎ 212/963-7713 🕐 Fri–Wed 9.15–4.45; closed weekends Jan–Feb 🍴 Restaurant
🚇 4, 5, 6, 7 42nd Street 🎟 Free

St Patrick's Cathedral

Trump Tower

Midtown

A stroll that takes you past all the greatest hits of Midtown.

DISTANCE: 2 miles (3km) **ALLOW:** 40 minutes (and more for Central Park)

START

MADISON SQUARE GARDEN
🚇 1, 2, 3 34th Street-Penn Station

END

ROCKEFELLER CENTER ▷ 62
🚇 B, D, F, V 47–50th Street/Rockefeller Center

❶ Take a look at Madison Square Garden, behind Penn Station a block west of the subway. Head back uptown, then take 34th Street east one block to Herald Square.

❽ If you have the energy and the time head north to Central Park for some more bucolic strolling.

❷ Macy's and Manhattan Mall are here. Toward the end of the next block, look up to your right. You're underneath the Empire State Building.

❼ Go west on 53rd Street, then south on Madison Avenue to 50th Street, and veer west. Here is Saks Fifth Avenue and St. Patrick's Cathedral, on the right. Straight ahead you'll find the vast Rockefeller Center.

❸ Head north up Fifth Avenue. Six blocks brings you to the Beaux-Arts magnificence of the New York Public Library, with Bryant Park behind.

❻ Circumnavigate Grand Central, hitting Park Avenue again at 46th Street, with the MetLife building at your back. A few blocks north are the precursors of the Manhattan skyline: Lever House and the Seagram Building.

❹ Pass the library, then go east on 42nd Street until you reach Grand Central Terminal. On the corner of Park Avenue is the Whitney's outpost in the Philip Morris Building.

❺ Continue east a block and a half and on the left is the Chrysler Building.

MIDTOWN

WALK

Shopping

BERGDORF GOODMAN

For the most sophisticated shopping experience in New York, the eight-floor fashion-for-lunching-ladies department store in the former Vanderbilt mansion takes the cake.
🕂 E9 ✉ 754 5th Avenue/57th Street ☎ 212/753-7300 🚇 N, R, W 5th Avenue/59th Street

COACH

The leather goods, starring handbags, purses and shoes aren't at all boringly preppy any more—not since design director Reed Krakoff took charge. Exciting shapes and colors change with the seasons. There are other branches.
🕂 E10 ✉ 620 5th Avenue/50th Street ☎ 212/675-6403 🚇 E, V 5th Avenue/53rd Street

FAO SCHWARZ

The near-legendary toy store has lost its iconic giant clockwork tower but gained a whole new lease of life. There are plenty of areas for kids to experiment with giant toys you have no intention of dragging home. Don't forget to dance on the piano from *Big*.
🕂 E9 ✉ 767 5th Avenue/58th Street ☎ 212/644-9400 🚇 N, R, W Fifth Avenue/59th Street

MACY'S

The sign outside says it's the largest store in the world, and by the time you've made your way across the nine block-long floors of this grandfather of all department stores, you'll believe them. Everything (including thousands of other shoppers) is here.
🕂 D12 ✉ 151 W34th Street at Herald Square ☎ 212/695-4400 🚇 B, D, F, N, R 34th Street

MANOLO BLAHNIK

Creations for the feet that are sought after by fashionistas and celebrities.
🕂 D10 ✉ 31 W54th Street ☎ 212/582-3077 🚇 E, V Fifth Avenue/53rd Street

MICHAEL C. FINA

Every bride wants her list at this exclusive purveyor of gifts and tableware.
🕂 E11 ✉ 545 5th Avenue ☎ 212/557-2500 🚇 4, 5, 6, 7 Grand Central

COLUMBUS CIRCLE

The closest thing to a mall in Manhattan, this splashy high-rise reclaimed drab Columbus Circle from the traffic when it opened in 2004. Upstairs are posh restaurants, plus the Mandarin Oriental hotel and a swanky health club. The lowest four levels contain the shopping experience. The *piece de resistance* is the below-ground-level Whole Foods Market (see right)—a Texan-born upscale grocery chain.

NIKE TOWN NY

Enter the Spaceship Sneaker and feel like a professional athlete. High-tech videos, multilevel displays and an industrial atmosphere encouraging aerobic shopping makes this popular with dads and their children.
🕂 C9 ✉ 11 Pennsylvania Plaza (57th Street) ☎ 212/946-2710 🚇 N, R 57th Street

TAKASHIMAYA

An austere Japanese esthetic informs the atmosphere of this small but exquisite department store. Housewares and gifts are the main focus but you'll stumble across other finds as well.
🕂 E9 ✉ 693 5th Avenue (55th Street) ☎ 212/350-0115 🚇 E, F 5th Avenue

WHOLE FOODS MARKET

The lower floor of the Time Warner Center is by far New York's largest food store. Find prepared food of every kind, hot bars of Indian, Latin and Asian dishes, cafés, a greenhouse for flowers, huge vitamins and natural cosmetics department, baked goods, fish, cheeses, meat, fruit…
🕂 C9 ✉ Concourse Level, Time Warner Center, Broadway (59th/60th Street) ☎ 212/823-9600 🚇 A, B, C, D, 1, 9 59th Street Columbus Circle

Entertainment and Nightlife

BIRDLAND
Big names, big bands, Coltrane tributes and Cubans is the range here.
🚼 C11 ✉ 315 W44th Street ☎ 212/581-3080 🚇 A, C, E 42nd Street Port Authority

CARNEGIE HALL
Considered one of the greatest recital halls in the world, featuring an eclectic program from classical artists to folk singers.
🚼 D9 ✉ 881 Seventh Avenue/57th Street ☎ 212/247-7800 🚇 N, R 57th Street; E Seventh Avenue

CAROLINE'S COMEDY CLUB
Established names and up-and-comers perform at this gold standard of clubs. Open every day.
🚼 C10 ✉ 1626 Broadway/ 49th Street ☎ 212/757-4100 🚇 1, 9 50th Street

ETHEL BARRYMORE THEATRE
Opened in 1928, this theater saw Fred Astaire perform in the 1930s just as his movie career was taking off.
🚼 C11 ✉ 243 West 47th Street ☎ 212/239-6200 🚇 1, 9, C, E 50th Street; N, R, W, 49th Street

FOUR SEASONS HOTEL
I.M. Pei's design gives this a sleek, austere energy. Impressive martini menu.
🚼 E9 ✉ 57 E57th Street (Lexington Avenue) ☎ 212/ 758-5700 🚇 4, 5, 6 59th Street

MADISON SQUARE GARDEN
The not-so-beautiful giant concrete circle is one of the city's major venues for music and sporting events. For the box office enter the Main Ticket Lobby at 7th Avenue and 32nd Street.
🚼 C13 ✉ 4 Pennsylvania Plaza ☎ 212/465-6741r 212/307-7171 (Ticketmaster) 🚇 1, 2, 3, 34th Street-Penn Station

THE NEW VICTORY THEATER
If you have kids of any age (over 5) in tow, there'll be something here to thrill them—and, chances are, you also. It has one of the best youth-centric programs.
🚼 C11 ✉ 209 W42nd Street/7th–8th Avenues ☎ 646/646-3020 or 646/562-2200 🚇 1, 2, 3, 7, N, R, Q, W Times Square

NIGHT CRAWLERS
Clubbing in New York is an art form. Most dance clubs don't get going until after midnight, and some don't stop until noon the next day. Friday and Saturday nights you'll see mostly suburbanites and tourists; die-hard New York clubbers prefer Sunday through Wednesday, when the ability to stay out all night is as much about status as it is about fun. Check weekly listings to see what's going on where.

NOKIA THEATRE
A medium-size venue for medium-big acts in the center of Times Square.
🚼 C11/D11 ✉ 1515 Broadway/44th Street ☎ 212/840-6800 🚇 1, 2, 3, 7, N, Q, R, S, W Times Square

OAK ROOM
A wood-panel classic in a famous hotel that's not what it was in Round Table days, but is still worth a visit for the Sunday jazz brunch and evening cocktails accompanied by torch singers and the like.
🚼 D11 ✉ Algonquin Hotel, 59 W445th Street /6th Avenue ☎ 212/840-6800 🚇 1B, D, F, V 42nd Street

RADIO CITY MUSIC HALL
This art deco theater, seating 5,882, was refurbished in 1999. You can take an hour-long tour and learn all about its life since it opened in 1932.
🚼 D10 ✉ 1260 6th Avenue at 50th Street ☎ 212/247-4777 🕐 Varied. Tours daily 11–3 🚇 B, D, F, V 40th–50th streets/ Rockefeller Center

ROSELAND BALLROOM
Nowadays mostly hosts indie bands, this 3,500-seat ballroom has been open continuously since 1919.
🚼 C10 ✉ 239 W52nd Street/Broadway ☎ 212/247-0200 🚇 B, D, E 7th Avenue

Restaurants

PRICES

Prices are approximate, based on a 3-course meal for one person.

$$$	over $60
$$	$40–$60
$	under $40

LE BERNARDIN ($$$)

Frenchman Eric Ripert is acknowledged to be the fish maestro. Exquisite, inventive dishes are served by waiters who practically polish your shoes.

🔒 D10 ✉ 155 W51st Street ☎ 212/489-7464 🚇 B, D, F, Q 47th–50th streets, Rockefeller Center

CAFÉ GRAY ($$)

Gray Kunz's successor to Lespinasse is the warmest space in the chilly Time Warner Center. His elevated bistro food is sublime.

🔒 C9 ✉ 10 Columbus Circle, 3rd floor/ 60th Street ☎ 212/823-6338 🚇 A, B, C, D, 1, 9 59th Streett/Columbus Circle

FOUR SEASONS ($$$)

Every once in a while a restaurant defines an age, and then transcends it. The Four Seasons changed the face of New York dining. Choose between the dark-wood-panel Grill Room and the romantic Pool Room.

🔒 E10 ✉ 99 E52nd Street ☎ 212/754-9494 🔵 Closed Sat lunch, Sun 🚇 6 51st Street

LEVER HOUSE ($$–$$$)

The mid-century-modern ocean liner-esque design by Mark Newman is the star at this ultra-glamorous restaurant downstairs in the iconic 1952 building on Park Avenue, but it would be worth visiting for chef Dan Silverman's eclectic-contempoprary menu alone.

🔒 E10 ✉ 390 Park Avenue/53rd Street ☎ 212/888-2700 🚇 E, V Lexington Avenue/53rd Street; 6 51st Street

THE MODERN ($$$)

With Danny Meyer (New York's best-loved restaurateur) in charge and young star chef, Alasatian born, Gabriel Kreuther behind the range, MoMA's fancy restaurant is not just for museum visits. Expect

TERMINAL FEEDING

Here are some highlights at the Food Court at Grand Central Terminal:
Café Spice for curries.
Caviarteria is as it sounds—fish eggs and champagne.
Custard Beach is all about the richest, bestest vanilla ice cream.
Junior's is a great diner with peerless cheesecake.
Knödel does wurst, boudin, merguez…
Mindy's Kosher Delicatessen does knishes and pastrami-on-rye.

fascinating takes on modern French food.

🔒 D10 ✉ 9 W53rd Street ☎ 212/333-1220 🚇 E, V Fifth Avenue/53rd Street

OYSTER BAR ($–$$)

Whether at the long counter or in the wood-paneled dining room, food in the 1913 vaulted Guastavino-tiled rooms in Grand Central is a thoroughly New York experience.

🔒 E11 ✉ Grand Central, lower level ☎ 212/490-6650 🚇 4, 5, 6, 7 Grand Central 42nd Street

PER SE ($$$)

If you want to know what all the fuss is about, reserve *way* ahead for French Laundry-maestro Thomas Keller's astonishing, precise and idiosyncratic food in one of the city's best-run rooms. A table by the window with those amazing views would be the top score.

🔒 C9 ✉ Time Warner Center, 10 Columbus Circle, 4th floor/60th Street ☎ 212/823-9335 🚇 A, B, C, D, 1, 2 59th Street/Columbus Circle

'21' CLUB ($$$)

This restaurant has been famous from its speakeasy days.

🔒 D10 ✉ 21 W52nd Street (Fifth/D106th avenues) ☎ 212/ 582-7200 🔵 Closed Sun 🚇 B, D, F 47th–50th streets

G G E N H E I M

Central Park is the city's lungs—a huge green space for all Manhattan. Visit the zoo; see free summer Shakespeare or bring a picnic. The museums of the Upper East Side are renowned worldwide.

Upper East Side & Central Park

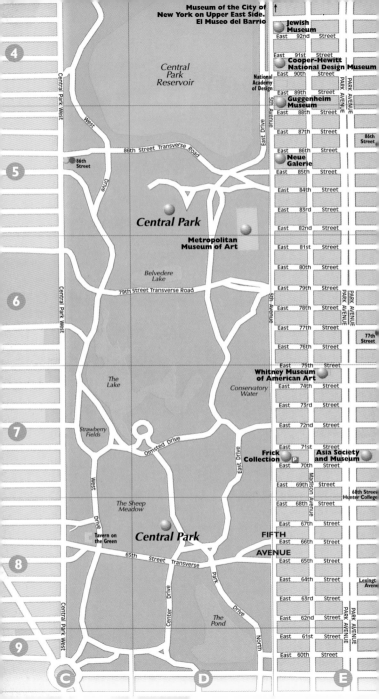

Museum of the City of
New York on Upper East Side.
El Museo del Barrio

Jewish Museum

East 92nd Street

East 91st Street
Cooper-Hewitt
National Design Museum

East 90th Street

National
Academy
of Design

East 89th Street
Guggenheim
Museum

East 88th Street

East 87th Street

86th
Street

East 86th Street

Neue
Galerie

East 85th Street

East 84th Street

East 83rd Street

East 82nd Street

Central Park

Metropolitan
Museum of Art

Central Park
Reservoir

West
Drive

86th Street Transverse Road

86th
Street

5

Belvedere Lake

79th Street Transverse Road

East 81st Street

East 80th Street

East 79th Street

5th Avenue

East 78th Street

6

PARK AVENUE
PARK AVENUE

East 77th Street

77th
Street

East 76th Street

East 75th Street

The Lake

Whitney Museum
of American Art

Conservatory
Water

East 74th Street

East 73rd Street

Strawberry
Fields

East 72nd Street

7

Olmsted drive

East Drive

East 71st Street

Frick
Collection

Asia Society
and Museum

East 70th Street

Madison Avenue

East 69th Street

68th Street
Hunter College

The Sheep
Meadow

East 68th Street

East 67th Street

Tavern on
the Green

Central Park

FIFTH

East 66th Street

AVENUE

65th Street Transverse

East 65th Street

8

East 64th Street

Lexingt
Avenue

Center Drive

East 63rd Street

Park Drive

East 62nd Street

PARK AVENUE
PARK AVENUE

The Pond

East 61st Street

North

East 60th Street

9

Central Park West

Central Park West

C

D

E

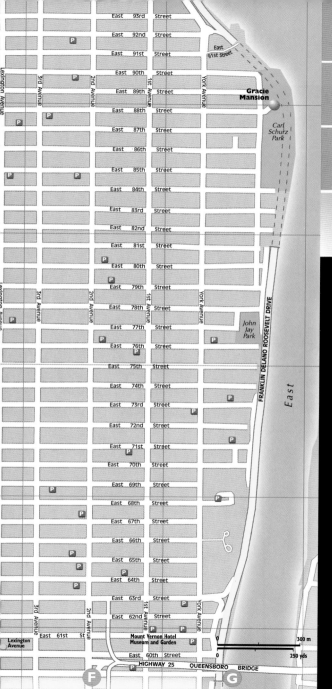

East 93rd Street
East 92nd Street
East 91st Street
East 90th Street
East 89th Street
East 88th Street
East 87th Street
East 86th Street
East 85th Street
East 84th Street
East 83rd Street
East 82nd Street
East 81st Street
East 80th Street
East 79th Street
East 78th Street
East 77th Street
East 76th Street
East 75th Street
East 74th Street
East 73rd Street
East 72nd Street
East 71st Street
East 70th Street
East 69th Street
East 68th Street
East 67th Street
East 66th Street
East 65th Street
East 64th Street
East 63rd Street
East 62nd Street
East 61st St
East 60th Street

East 91st Street

Lexington Avenue
3rd Avenue
2nd Avenue
1st Avenue
York Avenue

Gracie Mansion

Carl Schurz Park

John Jay Park

FRANKLIN DELANO ROOSEVELT DRIVE

East

Mount Vernon Hotel Museum and Garden

HIGHWAY 25   QUEENSBORO   BRIDGE

Lexington Avenue

F

G

0   300 m

0   250 yds

Upper East Side & Central Park

Central Park

TOP 25

HIGHLIGHTS

- Delacorte Theater, Shakespeare in the Park
- Summer stage concerts
- Bleachers at Heckscher
- Bethesda Fountain
- Wollman Rink in winter
- Strawberry Fields
- Swedish Cottage Marionette Theater
- Tavern on the Green

TIPS

- Don't walk alone in isolated areas at night.
- Watch out for bicycles on the roads.

The park is the escape valve for the city. Without it New York would overheat—especially in summer, when the humidity tops 90 percent, and bikers, runners, bladers, dog strollers and frisbee players convene. It's a way of life.

The Greensward Plan In the mid-19th century, when there was no Manhattan north of 42nd Street, New York Evening Post editor, William Cullen Bryant, campaigned until the city invested $5 million in an 840 acre (340ha) wasteland. Responsible for clearing the land was journalist Frederick Law Olmsted, who, with English architect Calvert Vaux, also won the competition to design the park, with his "Greensward Plan." By day, Olmsted supervised the clearance of 5 million cubic tons of dirt; by night, he and Vaux trod the

A variety of ways to enjoy the park; a view across the lake to the Dakota Building (below)

acres and designed. Nighttime walks, though no longer suicidal, are still not advised these days.

Fun and games Start at the Dairy Information Center and pick up a map and events list. These show the layout of the park and tell you about the Wildlife Conservation Center (Zoo), the Carousel, the playgrounds, rinks, fountains, statues and Strawberry Fields, where John Lennon is commemorated close to the Dakota Building where he lived and was shot. But the busy life of the park is not recorded on maps: rollerblade moves on the Mall by the Sheep Meadow; hanging out at the Heckscher Playground and Great Lawn softball leagues; doing the loop road by bike; sunbathing, poolside, at the vast Lasker Pool in Harlem; playing rowboat dodgems on the Lake; or bouldering on the outcrops of Manhattan schist (rock).

THE BASICS

www.centralparknyc.org

✚ D4–D9

☎ 212/794-6564 or 800/201-7275

🕐 Dairy Information Center Tue–Sun 10–5

🍽 Restaurants, kiosks

Ⓜ B, D, A, C Columbus Circle; 72, 81 96th Street; N, R 57th Street; B, Q 57th Street; 4, 5, 6 86th Street; 2, 3 110th Street

🚌 M1, M2, M3, M4, M5, M10, M18. Crosstown M66, M30, M72, M86

♿ Moderate

🆓 Free

Cooper-Hewitt

A detail and external view of the Cooper-Hewitt building

THE BASICS

www.ndm.si.edu

➕ E4

✉ 2 E91st Street

☎ 212/849-8420

🕐 Tue–Thu 10–5, Fri 10–9, Sat 10–6, Sun noon–6; closed holidays

🍴 None

🚇 4, 5, 6 86th Street

🚌 M1, M2, M3, M4

♿ Good

💲 Inexpensive

❓ Tours available

HIGHLIGHTS

● Paneling in the hall
● Solarium
● Garden
● Architectural drawings
● Summer concerts
● Textiles
● Exhibitions

TIP

● The Shop at Cooper-Hewitt is worth visiting in its own right. Many items from the changing stock are not available elsewhere and the book section is excellent.

The charming Cooper-Hewitt Design Museum collections are exhibited in an elegant, wood-paneled mansion. When snow falls in the holiday season, there's nowhere better to indulge in mawkishly nostalgic reveries.

Carnegie-Hewitt The mansion belonged to industrialist Andrew Carnegie, who, in 1903, had asked architects Babb, Cook & Willard for "the most modest, plainest and most roomy house in New York City." This he did not receive (aside from the roominess), since this little chateau was built with modern conveniences galore—air conditioning and elevators—and a big gated garden to keep out the squatter neighbors. The entire neighborhood came to be known as Carnegie Hill. Andrew's wife, Louise, lived here untill her death in 1946, then, some 20 years later, the Carnegie Corporation donated it to the Smithsonian Institution to house the Hewitt sisters' collections. The sisters, Amy, Eleanor and Sarah, had become infatuated with London's museums, and this set them collecting.

And Cooper The girls' grandpa Peter Cooper, founder of the Cooper Union college, housed the collection here, where it stayed until 1967. The contemporary Cooper-Hewitt is a vibrant institution where all kinds of events happen. Some of the collections are on display (it's hard to predict which) and there are reference resources, including the US's biggest architectural drawings collection and a textile library.

The Fifth Avenue garden (below) and Fragonard Room (right)

Frick Collection

Like the Wallace Collection in London and the Musée Picasso in Paris, Henry Clay Frick's mansion is half the reason for coming here. Henry bequeathed these riches to the nation as a memorial to himself—that's the kind of guy he was.

The mansion, and the man   Henry Clay Frick was chairman of the Carnegie Steel Corp. (US Steel). He was one of the most ruthless strike-breakers of all time and the nastiest industrialist of his day. Instead of any comeuppance (though there were assassination attempts), he got to commission Carrère and Hastings to build him one of the last great Beaux-Arts mansions on 5th Avenue and fill it with an exquisite collection of 14th- to 19th-century old masters, porcelain, furniture and bronzes. You can rest in a Louis XVI chair before strolling in the central glass-roofed courtyard and the gorgeous garden.

What Frick bought   Some of the 40 rooms are arranged around a particular work or artist, notably the Boucher Room, east of the entrance, and the Fragonard Room, with the 11-painting *Progress of Love* series. There are British masters (Constable, Gainsborough, Whistler, Turner), Dutch (Vermeer, Rembrandt, Van Eyck, Hals), Italian (Titian, Bellini, Veronese) and Spanish (El Greco, Goya, Velázquez). Interspersed are Limoges enamel and Chinese porcelain, Persian carpets and Marie Antoinette's furniture. Some Frick descendants still have keys to this modest pied à terre, which has a bowling alley in the basement.

THE BASICS

www.frick.org

➕ E7

✉ 1 E70th Street

☎ 212/288–0700

🕐 Tue–Sat 10–6, Sun 11–5; closed holidays

🚇 6 68th Street

🚌 M1, M2, M3, M4

♿ Good

💷 Moderate

❓ Lectures: Wed 5.30

HIGHLIGHTS

● *Mall in St. James' Park*, Gainsborough (1783)
● *Sir Thomas More*, Holbein (1527)
● *Officer and the Laughing Girl*, Vermeer (1655–60)
● *The Polish Rider*, Rembrandt (c1655)
● *Virgin and Child with Saints*, Van Eyck (c1441–43)
● *Philip IV of Spain*, Velázquez (1644)

UPPER EAST SIDE & CENTRAL PARK

★ TOP 25

TOP 25

HIGHLIGHTS

- The building
- *L'Hermitage à Pontoise,* Pissarro (1867)
- *Paris Through the Window,* Chagall (1913)
- *Woman Ironing,* Picasso (1904)
- *Nude,* Modigliani (1917)
- Kandinskys
- Klees
- Légers
- The store

If you just happened across Frank Lloyd Wright's space-age rotunda, your eyes would pop out of their sockets, but it's the planet's best-known modern building, so you are prepared. Don't forget the art inside.

Museum of architecture This is the great Frank Lloyd Wright's only New York building. It was commissioned by Solomon R. Guggenheim at the urging of his friend and taste tutor, Baroness Hilla Rebay von Ehrenwiesen, though the wealthy metal-mining magnate died 10 years before it was completed in 1959. The giant white nautilus is certainly arresting but it's the interior that unleashes the most superlatives. Take the elevator to the top level and snake your way down the museum's spiral ramp to see why. You can study the exhibits,

A variety of pictures that demonstrate the stunning design by Frank Lloyd Wright

look over the parapet to the lobby below and finish up where you began.

Museum of art   There are around 6,000 pieces in the Guggenheim Foundation's possession. Solomon R. and his wife Irene Rothschild abandoned the old masters they sought at first, when Hilla Rebay introduced them to Léger, Kandinsky, Mondrian and Moholy-Nagy, Chagall and Gleizes, and they got hooked on the moderns. See also the early Picassos in the small rotunda and the 1992 tower extension. If you like the Impressionists and Postimpressionists, look for the Thannhauser Collection, always on display—unlike the rotated Guggenheim holdings. Plans for the new Guggenheim museum, designed by Frank Gehry on Piers 9, 11, 13 and 14 on the East River in Lower Manhattan, are on hold.

THE BASICS

www.guggenheim.org/
new_york
✚ E4
✉ 1071 5th Avenue (88th Street)
☎ 212/423-3500
🕐 Sat–Wed 10–5.45, Fri 10–7.45; closed Dec 25
🍽 Café
Ⓠ 4, 5, 6 86th Street
🚌 M1, M2, M3, M4
♿ Good
💰 Moderate–expensive
❓ Lecture program

TIP

● Consider a City Pass ($63; kids $46). As well as the Gugg, it allows entry to other leading attractions. Visit www.citypass.com for information.

Metropolitan Museum of Art

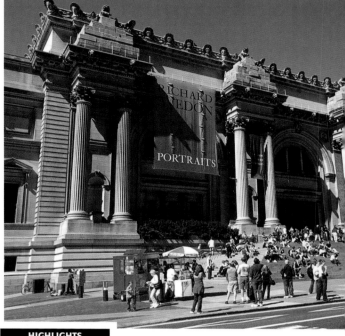

HIGHLIGHTS

● Temple of Dendur (15BC)
● Period rooms, American Wing
● *Young Woman with a Water Jug*, Vermeer (1660–67)
● *Venus and Adonis*, Rubens (1630s)
● *Grand Canal, Venice*, Turner (c1835)

TIP

● Consider visiting on Friday or Saturday evening, when a string quartet serenades you and there are far fewer crowds.

It will give you bigger blisters than the Uffizi, bigger chills than the Sistine Chapel and take a bigger slice of vacation time than all dinners. It's so big that it doesn't just contain Egyptian artifacts but an entire Egyptian building.

Art city The limestone Beaux-Arts facade with its tremendous steps was a 1902 addition to the Calvert Vaux (of Central Park fame) redbrick Gothic building buried inside. There are several more buildings-within-buildings, interior gardens and courtyards, such is the scale of the Met. The 15BC Temple of Dendur, in its glass-walled bemoated chamber east of the main entrance on the upper floor, is the best known, but there's much more besides: the Astor Court above it—a replica Ming dynasty scholar's courtyard—plus, in

The outside steps on a busy summer day (left); inside the main entrance of the museum with the information desk at the center (below)

the American Wing, a score of period-style rooms, and the vast and sunlighted garden court with its hodgepodge of Tiffany glass and topiary, a Frank Lloyd Wright window and the entire Federal-style facade of the United States Bank from Wall Street.

Where to start? How to stop? A quarter of the 3 million-plus objects are up at any one time, so pace yourself. Relax. There are about 15 discrete collections. Some visitors decide on one or two per visit—13th- to 18th-century European Paintings (or part thereof) and Ancient Art, perhaps—and leave it at that. Or you could structure a route around one or two favorite and familiar works. On the gound level, the Information Center in the Uris Center, with its Orientation Theater and giant floor plans, is the place to begin, whatever you decide to see.

THE BASICS

www.metmuseum.org

➕ D5

✉ 1000 Fifth Avenue (82nd Street)

☎ 212/535-7710

🕐 Tue–Thu, Sun 9.30–5.15, Fri, Sat 9.30–8.45

🍴 Cafeteria, restaurant, bar

🚇 4, 5, 6 86th Street

🚌 M1, M2, M3, M4

♿ Good

👎 Moderate

❓ The Cloisters (▷ 106) houses more of the Met's medieval collections; same-day admission on Met ticket

HIGHLIGHTS

● Biennial
● *Circus*, Alexander Calder (1926–31)
● The Hoppers
● The O'Keeffes
● *Dempsey and Firpo*, George Bellows (1924)
● The Louise Nevelsons
● Drawbridge

TIP

● Come Fridays from 6pm to 9pm. Admission is pay-what-you-wish and there are live musical performances.

More modern than the Modern, the Whitney wants to be as unpredictable as the artist du jour and very often succeeds. It's a New York tradition to sneer at the Biennial, whether or not one has seen the show.

No room at the Met Sculptor and patron of her contemporaries' work, Gertrude Vanderbilt Whitney offered her collection to the Met in 1929, but the great institution turned up its nose and Whitney was forced to found the Whitney. In 1966, Marcel Breuer's cantilevered, granite-clad Brutalist block was completed to house it in a suitably controversial manner and here it lours still, not universally loved but impossible to overlook. The Whitney's core collection now reads like a roll call of American 20th-century greats: Edward Hopper,

Vivisos at the information and entry desks at the Whitney

Thomas Hart Benton, Willem de Kooning, Georgia O'Keeffe, Claes Oldenburg, Jasper Johns, George Bellows, Jackson Pollock are a few. Let's hope the curators and buyers are as good as Gertrude at spotting talent.

Take your pick Exhibitions, drawn from the museum's important and delicious collection, often emphasize a single artist's work. At other times they prove more eclectic. There's an active film and video department, and a branch in Park Avenue. There were four branches in Manhattan alone during the art boomtime of the 1980s. The Whitney Biennial (in the spring of even-numbered years) offers an echo of those days, when the New York art pack gets sweaty debating the merits and demerits of the chosen few on show and of the curator's vision.

THE BASICS

www.whitney.org
➕ E7
✉ 945 Madison Avenue (75th Street)
☎ 212/570-3676
🕐 Wed–Thu, Sat–Sun 11–6, Fri 1–9; closed Thanksgiving, Dec 25, Jan 1
🍴 Café
🚇 6 77th Street
🚌 M1, M2, M3, M4
♿ Good
💰 Moderate
❓ Lectures, video/film:
Whitney at the Philip Morris Building
✉ Park Avenue (42nd Street) ☎ 212/663-2453
🕐 Wed–Thu 11–6, Fri 1–9, Sat–Sun 11–6; closed Thanksgiving, Dec 25, Jan 1

More to See

ASIA SOCIETY
This collection of Asian art and culture is based on that started by John D. Rockefeller III. The society was founded in 1956 and moved to its present headquarters in the 1980s.
➕ E7 ✉ 725 Park Avenue (70th Street)
☎ 212/288-6400 🕐 Closed Mon
🚇 6 68th Street 💲 Inexpensive

GRACIE MANSION
Gracie Mansion has been the mayor's official residence since 1942 though Mayor Bloomberg declined it. When it was built in 1799, this was a remote country house.
➕ G4 ✉ East End Avenue (88th Street)
🚇 4, 5, 6 86th Street

JEWISH MUSEUM
The largest Jewish museum in the Western hemisphere chronicling Jewish experience worldwide, with artifacts from 4,000 years ago.
➕ E4 ✉ 1109 5th Avenue/92nd Street
☎ 212/423-3200 🕐 Sun–Wed 11–5.45, Thu 11–8, Fri 11–3 🍴 Café F4, 5, 6 86th Street 💲 Inexpensive

MUSEO DEL BARRIO
New York's only museum dedicated to Latin American and Caribbean art and culture. The collection has 8,000 items and stages regular exhibitions.
➕ Off map at E4 ✉ 1230 Fifth Avenue (104th Street) ☎ 212/831-7272
🕐 Wed–Sun 11–5 🚇 6 103rd Street
💲 Donation

MUSEUM OF THE CITY OF NEW YORK
Rotating exhibitions that illustrate the changing life of the city dating back to 1624. Special walking tours available.
➕ Off map at E4 ✉ 1220 Fifth Avenue (103rd Street) ☎ 212/534-1672
🕐 Wed–Sat 10–5, Sun noon–5 🚇 6 103rd Street 💲 Free (contribution)

NEUE GALERIE NEW YORK
Dedicated to early 20th-century German and Austrian art and design, this gallery has marvelous collections of paintings and other media.
➕ E5 ✉ 1048 Fifth Avenue (86th Street)
☎ 212/628-6200 🕐 Fri, Sat, Mon 11–7, Sun 1–6 🚇 4, 5, 6 86th Street 💲 Moderate

Museum of the City of New York

Gracie Mansion

Shopping

BARNEYS
Many are the New Yorkers who dress exclusively from the *ne plus ultra* of high-fashion stores. Over several floors find avant garde designers, own label clothes, the city's best high-end cosmetics and scent departments, every hip jeans label, menswear, epic shoe departments, directional jewelry, homewares, kids' clothes and more. Prices are high.
⊞ E9 ✉ 660 Madison Avenue/61st Street ☎ 212/826-8900 Ⓜ N, R, W Fifth Avenue/59th Street

BLOOMINGDALE'S
Bloomingdale's, opened in 1879, is one of the most venerable names in Manhattan yet keeps up with every trend. The jewelry and handbag sections are excellent.
⊞ F9 ✉ 1000 Third Avenue at 59th Street ☎ 212/705-2000 or 212/729-5900 Ⓜ 4, 6 59th Street; N, R Prince Street

CALVIN KLEIN
The iconic New York designer's flagship store, designed by David Chipperfield, is as spare and minimal as his clothing without even racks to spoil the clean lines (you point at a display and request your size). His home line is downstairs.
⊞ E9 ✉ 654 Madison Avenue/60th Street ☎ 212/292-9000 Ⓜ N, R, W 5th Avenue/59th Street

CRATE & BARREL
Having refreshed your wardrobe come here for the wardrobe itself, perhaps in cherrywood? Fashionable housewares and furniture at reasonable prices made New Yorkers adopt this national chain as their own.
⊞ E9 ✉ Madison Avenue at 59th Street ☎ 212/308- 0011 Ⓜ N, R Fifth Avenue

DONNA KARAN
This beautiful bi-level space carries the home line, accessories and the best of new season Karan, as well as her lower-price lines.
⊞ E9 ✉ 819 Madison Avenue at 60th Street ☎ 212/861-1001 Ⓜ N, R, W Fifth Avenue/59th Street

KITCHEN ARTS AND LETTERS
A treasure trove of cookbooks by leading authors including James beard and Julia Child.
⊞ E4 ✉ 1435 Lexington Avenue between 93rd and 94th streets ☎ 212/876-5550 Ⓜ 6 96th Street

RALPH LAUREN
Distinguished cowboy and English country heritage looks in the Rhinelander Mansion, one of a few of such turn-of-the-20th-century houses in Manhattan
⊞ E7 ✉ 867 Madison Avenue between E. 71st and 72nd streets ☎ 212/606-2100 Ⓜ 6 68th Street

SHANGHAI TANG
Youthful Asian-style clothing.
⊞ E8 ✉ 714 Madison Avenue between E. 63rd and 64th streets ☎ 212/888-0111 Ⓜ 4, 5, 6, F Lexington Avenue

ZITOMER
At root, an über-drugstore, this Upper East Side classic has grown to encompass everything from toys to pet accessories. The number and scope of bath, body and skincare ranges is impressive and it's hands-down the best place to shop for hair ornaments (okay, maybe a tie with Ricky's).
⊞ E6 ✉ 969 Madison Avneue/76th Street ☎ 212/737-2016 Ⓜ 6 77th Street

Entertainment and Nightlife

92ND STREET Y

A wonderfully varied program of events here includes readings by renowned authors, folk, jazz and lectures that cover a wide range of subjects. Celebrated its 125th anniversary in 1999.

➕ E4 ✉ Kauffman Concert Hall, 1395 Lexington Avenue at 92nd Street ☎ 212/415-5500 🚇 6 96th Street

CAFÉ CARLYLE

This lounge in the elegant Carlyle Hotel was home to the great Bobby Short, until his death in 2005, but his spirit lives on in the booking policy: piano player lounge singers. Do look in at Bemeleman's Bar.

➕ E6 ✉ Carlyle Hotel, Madison Avenue /76th Street ☎ 212/570-7189 🚇 6 68th Street

CAFÉ PIERRE

Jazz and cabaret songs, plus requests, from Nancy Winston and Kathleen Landis.

➕ E9 ✉ Fifth Avenue at 61st Street ☎ 212/940-8185 🚇 N, R, W Fifth Avenue/59th Street

DANGERFIELD'S

This club, established in 1969 is going strong. Those who have performed here include Jay Leno, Jim Carrey and Tim Allen.

➕ E8 ✉ 15 East 65th Street ☎ 212/734-2130 🚇 6 68th Street

FEINSTEINS AT THE REGENCY

The cabaret star Michael Feinstein himself performs at his namesake venue only a couple of times a year but the rest of the time he manages to secure top Broadway names for this swanky, initmate room.

➕ E9 ✉ Regency Hotel, 540 Park Avenue/61st Street ☎ 212/339-4095 🚇 N, R, W Lexington Avenue/59th Street

FLORENCE GOULD HALL

The 400-seat venue is associated with the Alliance Française. The range of events encompasses opera, jazz and pop singers, dance and readings.

➕ E9 ✉ 55 E59th Street (Park and Madison avenues) ☎ 212/355-6160 🚇 N, R, W Fifth Avenue/59th Street

---

OUT IN CENTRAL PARK

Central Park is a welcoming park. For those who crave physical activity there's lots to do.

Bike Riding You can rent no-frills bicycle.

Roller Blading Skate rental and lessons are available at Wollman Rink.

Ice Skating Wollman Rink rents figure skates and hockey skates and is an ice rink in winter.

Running The most popular place for running and jogging.

GRACE RAINEY ROGERS AUDITORIUM

A 700-seat auditorium in the Met for musical groups. Chamber music is also played in the great hall balcony of the Met on Friday and Saturday evenings.

➕ D5 ✉ Metropolitan Museum of Art, 5th Avenue at 52nd Street ☎ 212/535-7710 or 212/570-3949 🚇 6 77th Street

THE IRIS AND B. GERALD CANTOR ROOF GARDEN

You can get cocktails and simple food on this rooftop terrace with bits of its sponsors' sculpture collection casually strewn among the wisteria trellises and a heavenly view of Central Park treetops. It's one of the nicest places for an early drink in New York. Access is via the elevators on the far southwest corner. It's open until 4.30pm; 8.30pm Friday and Saturday.

➕ D5 ✉ Metropolitan Museum of Art, 1000 5th Avenue/82nd Street ☎ 212/535-7710 🚇 6 86th Street

THEATER TENTEN

A rare Upper East Side off-Broadway theater. Productions range from Gilbert and Sullivan to poetry readings.

➕ E5 ✉ 1010 Park Avenue 85th Street ☎ 212/288-3246 🚇 6 86th Street

Restauntants

PRICES

Prices are approximate, based on a 3-course meal for one person.

$$$	over $60
$$	$40–$60
$	under $40

BOAT HOUSE ($$)

Leave Manhattan entirely at this unique lakeside place in the depths of Central Park. The food is contemporary American and it's fine but the view is the point. There's also a separate cocktail deck that gets predictably mobbed after office hours in summer.

➕ D7 ✉ Central Park, near-est to E72nd Street entrance ☎ 212/517-2233 🕐 Closed major holidays 🚇 6 68th Street-Hunter College

CAFÉ BOULUD ($$$)

Many diners consider this to be their favorite Daniel Boulud restaurant. Three Daniel muses inspire the menu—classics, seasons and ethnic cuisines. You will find a pot au feu, a good bouillabaisse and entrées inspired by Tuscany, Morocco, Vietnam and Spain.

➕ E6 ✉ 20 East 76th Street ☎ 212/772-2600 🕐 Closed major holidays 🚇 6 77th Street

CAFÉ SABARSKY ($–$$)

Much more than a museum café, this—

fittingly for somewhere in the patrician town house that is the Neue Galerie—looks like a 1920s Viennese Kafeehaus and has New York's premier Austrian chef, Kurt Gutenbrunner at the helm. You can also just drop in for the *Kaffee und Kuchen.*

➕ E5 ✉ Neue Galerie, 1048 Fifth Avenue/86th Street ☎ 212/288-0665 🕐 Closed major holidays 🚇 4, 5, 6 786h Street

DANIEL ($$$)

Perhaps the most formal restaurant in the city, with its salmon-pink walls and columned arches. Serves exquisitely restrained, modern French dishes—opt for the degustation menu to fully appreciate chef Daniel Boulud's brilliance. Dessert arrives with its own "basket" of

TAVERN ON THE GREEN

The Tavern delivers a memorable dining experience despite its stature as a tourist destination, and despite the breadth of its menu which ranges from prime rib with Yorkshire pudding to sautéed rainbow trout in brown butter sauce. In summer you can dance under the stars in the garden from 9pm.

➕ C8 ✉ Central Park West at 67th Street ☎ 212/873-3200 🚇 1, 9 66th Street

warm madeleines.

➕ E8 ✉ 60 E65th Street (Madison/Park avenues) ☎ 212/288-0033 🕐 Closed Sun 🚇 6 68th Street

JACKSON HOLE ($)

This small chain of burger places is so useful when all you want is a hefty sandwich in a child-friendly, no-frills environment after a long day hitting the museums.

➕ E4 ✉ 1270 Madison Avenue/91st Street ☎ 212/427-2820 🚇 4, 5, 6 86th Street

➕ F8 ✉ 232 E64th Street/2nd Avenue ☎ 212/371-7187 🕐 Closed major holidays 🚇 6 68th Street/Hunter College

SERENDIPITY 3 ($)

So what if it's a cliché? This toy box/candy store of an Upper East Side institution makes the original and best "Frozen Hot Chocolate." You don't even need a child in tow but you do need a sweet tooth—and the rest of the menu is forgettable.

➕ F9 ✉ 225 E60th Street/2nd Avenue ☎ 212/838-3531 🚇 4, 5, 6 59th Street

SUSHI OF GARI ($$$)

One of the newer high-end sushi places is always full, despite high prices. Say *Omakase* to chef Gari and sharpen your tastebuds.

➕ F6 ✉ 402 E78th Street/1st Avenue ☎ 212/517-5340 🚇 6 77th Street

West of Central Park is a largely residential, pleasantly leafy neighborhood of grand apartment buildings and big brownstones. Its major attraction is Lincoln Center, with world-class performances.

Central
Park
Reservoir

West
Drive

East Drive

86th Street Transverse Road

Central Park

Metropolitan
Museum of Art

Belvedere
Lake

79th Street Transverse Road

5th Avenue

The
Lake

Conservatory
Water

Olmsted Drive

East Drive

The Sheep
Meadow

Central Park

65th Street Transverse

Park
Drive

Center Drive

The
Pond

North

| 0 | | 300 m |
| 0 | | 250 yds |

D

E

American Museum of Natural History

HIGHLIGHTS

- Blue whale
- Barosaurus
- Herd of stuffed elephants
- New dinosaur halls
- Sky Shows
- Star of India
- The dioramas
- Dinosaur embryo
- "Starry Nights" jazz at the Rose Center

TIP

- You can observe the entire life cycle of tropical butterflies from October to June at the Butterfly Conservatory.

No longer a lovable anachronism since its renovation, this 19th-century hulk is stuffed with dinosaur skeletons and appended by the amazing Rose Center. The blue whale's cocktail bar and the dioramas are delightful.

Who's who Of the 36 million items owned by the museum—the largest such institution in the world—only a small fraction is on show. Among the improvements funded by a $45-million cash injection were a sprucing-up of the buildings themselves and, most notably, the metamorphosed Hayden Planetarium, now the Rose Center, next door, with its thrill ride through the universe. Another highlight is the partially interactive dinosaurs to please computer-jaded children. There's far too much to see in one day, with three

The dinosaurs are always popular, especially with children visiting the museum (left); the entrance of the museum (below)

city blocks and the entire evolution of life on earth covered. Not-to-be-missed items include the barosaurus rearing up to her full 55ft (17m) to protect her young from a T-rex attack and the 94ft (29m) blue whale that dominates the two-story Hall of Ocean Life and Biology of Fishes.

More gems   Another highlight is the 563-carat Star of India sapphire, part of the unbelievable Hall of Meteorites, Minerals and Gems, containing almost $50-million worth of precious stones, plus the 34-ton Ahnighito meteorite. The cutest part of the museum is where animals of all sizes are displayed behind glass in *tableaux morts* of great artistic merit. In the Nature Max theater a four-story screen shows ecological blockbusters but it's the new planetarium, a dramatic 87ft (27m) sphere in a glass cube, that takes the cake.

THE BASICS

www.amnh.org

✚ C6

✉ Central Park West (79th Street)

☎ 212/769-5100

🕐 Daily 10–5.45

🍴 Various

🚇 B, C 81st Street

🚌 M7, M10, M11, M79

♿ Good

💲 Moderate to expensive

❓ 75-min tours until 3.15. Rose Center jazz and tapas first Friday of month

☎ 212/769-5200

Lincoln Center

HIGHLIGHTS

● Chandeliers in the Met auditorium
● Reflecting Pool with Henry Moore's Reclining Figure (1965)
● Lincoln Center Out-of-Doors Festival
● NY City Ballet's Nutcracker
● Chagall murals, Met foyer
● Thursday morning rehearsals, Avery Fisher Hall
● New York Film Festival
● Philip Johnson's Plaza fountain
● Jazz at Lincoln Center
● Annual Messiah singalong

TIP

● Dance under the stars at the Midsummer Night's Swing in Josie Robertson Plaza, a free summertime series of live band sessions.

Strolling to the fantastically fairy-lighted ten-story Metropolitan Opera House colonnade across the Central Plaza on a winter's night is one of the most glamorous things you can do in this city, and you don't need tickets.

West Side Story The Rockefeller-funded über-arts center was envisaged in the late 1950s and finished in 1969, after 7,000 families and 800 businesses had been pushed aside by developer Robert Moses and the John D. Rockefeller millions. Much of *West Side Story* was filmed here after the demolition began.

All the arts The 15 acres (6ha) include mega-houses for the biggest-scale arts, all designed by different architects in the same white travertine.

Lincoln Center at night (left) and with the Christmas decorations glowing (below)

THE BASICS

www.lincolncenter.org

✚ B8

✉ Broadway (62nd–67th streets)

☎ 212/546-2656
Met 212/362-6000
Avery Fisher Hall
212/875-5030
Jazz 212/258-9800

🕐 Inquire for performance times

🍴 Restaurants, cafés, bars

🚇 1, 9 66th Street Lincoln Center

🚌 M5, M7, M104, crosstown M66

♿ Good

🎟 Admission to Center free

❓ Tours leave from concourse under Met, daily 10–5 ☎ 212/875-5350

The Metropolitan Opera House is the glamor queen, with her vast Marc Chagall murals, miles of red carpet, swooshes of stair and starry chandeliers that silently and thrillingly rise to the sky-high gold-leaf ceiling before performances. Avery Fisher Hall caught America's oldest orchestra, the NY Philharmonic, on its trajectory out of Carnegie Hall, while the Juilliard School of Music supplies it with fresh maestri. The New York State Theater, housing the New York City Opera and the New York City Ballet, faces Avery Fisher across the Plaza. In 2004, the Rose Theater opened as the centerpiece of Jazz at Lincoln Center in the Time Warner Center. Two smaller theaters, the Vivian Beaumont and Mitzi Newhouse, and a more intimate concert hall, Alice Tully, plus the Walter Reade movie theater and the little Bruno Walter Auditorium, complete the pack.

Upper West Side

The Upper West Side is famous for its grand apartment buildings.

DISTANCE: 1.5 miles (2.5km)   **ALLOW:** 40 minutes

THE DAKOTA
🚇 B, C 72nd Street

1 Start at the Dakota on the north-west corner of Central Park West and 72nd Street. John Lennon lived and died here. Cross Central Park West to see the Strawbery Fields memorial.

2 Return to Central Park West and turn left. Walk south to West 65th Street. Turn right and walk west toward Broadway. Cross to Lincoln Center.

3 Explore Lincoln Center and its pleasant open-air areas. Then head to the steps of the Julliard School and turn right, then left onto Broadway. Re-cross Broadway.

4 Turn left onto Columbus. Walk north toward 70th Street past the ABC Building. At West 70th Street turn left and head west to 135 West 70th Street.

END

AMERICAN MUSEUM OF NATURAL HISTORY 🚇 B, C 72nd Street

8 Cross 77th Street and you'll have arrived at the American Museum of Natural History. Allow lots of time for your visit here.

7 Walk north and you'll pass the San Remo Apartments (former residents include Paul Simon and Dustin Hoffman). Keep on north to the New-York Historical Society on the corner of 77th Street. The shop here has interesting gifts.

6 Continue to Amsterdam Avenue and then turn right. Ahead, the Ansonia Building stands between Broadway and West 73rd and 74th streets. Next head right on West 73rd Street back to Central Park West and the Dakota again.

5 Admire the cobalt blue glass of the art deco Pythian Temple, a masonic lodge turned apartment building.

WALK

UPPER WEST SIDE

Shopping

ALPHABETS
A small store crammed with *tchotchkes* for the home—cocktail paraphernalia, smelly candles, dishes—and hipster clothes, most of it amusing.
✚ B5 ✉ 2284 Broadway/82nd Street ☎ 212/579-5702 🚇 1,2 79th Street

BARNES AND NOBLE
This is one of the megabook chain's main New York branches. There's usually an evening reading.
✚ B5 ✉ 2289 Broadway/82nd Street ☎ 212/362-8835, and branches 🚇 1, 9 79th Street

BETSEY JOHNSON
This long-lived fashion darling produces fun looks.
✚ C7 ✉ 248 Columbus Avenue/71st Street ☎ 212/362-3364 🚇 1, 2, 3 72nd Street

FAIRWAY
Get a taste of Upper West Side everyday life at this bewilderingly comprehensive grocery.
✚ B6 ✉ 2127 Broadway/75th Street ☎ 212/595-1888 🚇 1, 9, 2, 3 72nd Street

FISHS EDDY
The crockery and glassware at amazing prices is adorned with logos from ocean liners, vintage nightclubs and the like, though it's all "dead stock"—i.e., never used.

There are also original ranges.
✚ B6 ✉ 2176 Broadway/77th Street ☎ 212/873-8819 🚇 1, 2 79th Street

LAILA ROWE
This is one of a growing chain-ette of accessories stores, crammed with colorful gear. Expect a fun vibe and fast-changing selections of jewelry at prices that belie their on-the-money directional style.
✚ C7 ✉ 253 Columbus Avenue/72nd Street ☎ 212/579-5254 🚇 B, C, 1, 2, 3 72nd Street

MALIA MILLS
The boutique swimwear emporium cherished by every woman who's ever loathed her reflection: there are mix-and-match pieces made to fit everyone—and they're super-cool, too.

SUMMER IN THE CITY
One of the best reasons to brave the summer heat is for the wonderful selection of free entertainment put on by many of the city's premier cultural institutions. Without paying a dime it's possible to enjoy alfresco operas, theater, art, eating, jazz, classical music, movies, dance, rock-and-roll, blues and folk music. Many arrive early for big performances and stake out a spot for a picnic.

✚ C7 ✉ 220 Columbus Avenue/70th Street ☎ 212/874-7200 🚇 B, C 72nd Street/1, 2, 3 72nd Street

PATAGONIA
If you like social and environmentally consciousness with your outdoor wear but still want to look slick while climbing the mountain, swimming the Channel or just looking like you might have done so, then this is your place.
✚ B6 ✉ 426 Columbus Avenue/80th Street ☎ 917/441-0011 🚇 B, C 81st Street–Museum of Natural History

STEVEN ALAN
The Lower East Side look on the Upper Wests Side: this is a carefully edited array of the most cutting-edge small hipsters' labels, some of them available nowhere else—including Alan's own.
✚ B5 ✉ 465 Amsterdam Avenue/82nd Street ☎ 212/595-8451 🚇 1, 2 86th Street

ZABAR'S
This is the pleasingly wise-cracking New Yawker of the foodie havens with a Jewish soul all its own. Cheese, coffee, smoked fish and the like are downstairs, while upstairs are the city's best buys in kitchenwares.
✚ B6 ✉ 2245 Broadway/80th Street ☎ 212/787-2000 🚇 1, 9 79th Street

UPPER WEST SIDE

🏬

SHOPPING

Entertainment and Nightlife

AMSTERDAM BILLIARDS + BAR

A world of pool with drinks until the small hours. Everyone plays at this 30-table cavern, from idiots to pros. Rent a table or just watch.

➕ B6 ✉ 344 Amsterdam Avenue/76th Street ☎ 212/496-8180 🚇 1, 2 79th Street

AVERY FISHER HALL

The home of the New York Philharmonic seats 2,700. The hall is also home to other groups including the American Symphony Orchestra.

➕ B8 ✉ 111 Amsterdam Avenue between West 64th and 65th streets ☎ 212/875-5030 or 212/721-6500 🚇 1, 9 66th Street

BEACON THEATRE

Storytelling, readings, children's performance, music, dance and more.

➕ B7 ✉ 2124 Broadway/74th Street ☎ 212/496-7070 or 212/307-7171 🚇 1, 2, 3, 9 72nd Street

BRUNO WALTER AUDITORIUM

Seminars, lectures, films and concerts.

➕ B6 ✉ The New York Library for the Performing Arts, 111 Amsterdam Avenue between 64th and 65th streets ☎ 212/870-1630 or 212/642-0142 🚇 1, 9 66th Street

DIZZY'S CLUB COCO COLA

The new Jazz at Lincoln Center's even newer club is, in the spirit of Dizzy (Gillespie—who else?), designed to make performers and spectators alike *relaaaaax*. The Monday night "Upstairs" series is popular; there are also After Hours Sets Tuesday through Saturday nights.

➕ C9 ✉ Broadway/60th Street, 5th floor ☎ 212/258-9595 🚇 A, B, C, D, 1, 2 59th Street/Columbus Circle

LINCOLN PLAZA CINEMAS

Six screens showing successful first runs and foreign movies.

➕ B8 ✉ 1886 Broadway/63rd Street ☎ 212/757-2280 🚇 1, 9 66th Street

MAKOR

A wide variety of music, plus other events are here at this annex of the 92nd Street Y, designed for those in their 20s and 30s.

BIG IN NEW YORK

From the elegance of a grand opera to the excitement of avant-garde performance art, New York spectacles are world-class (even the flops). Broadway shows can be expensive, but nothing transports like a great multimillion-dollar musical or an intense performance by a drama diva.

Be sure to reserve tickets in advance for the most popular shows.

➕ C8 ✉ 35 West 67th Street/ Columbus Avenue ☎ 212/601-1000 🚇 1, 9 66th Street

THE METROPOLITAN OPERA

The gala openings at this world-class opera rank among the most glamorous of the city's cultural events. Serious buffs line up on Saturday mornings for inexpensive standing-room tickets. The season runs October to April.

➕ B8 ✉ Lincoln Center ☎ 212/362-6000 🚇 1, 9 66th Street

NEW YORK CITY OPERA

The Met's neighbor, the repertoire of this fine opera company incorporates a wider variety including newer works, operetta and musicals.

➕ B8 ✉ Lincoln Center ☎ 212/870-5570 🚇 1, 9 66th Street

STAND UP NEW YORK

Traditional comedy club where new and aspiring comics test their routines.

➕ B6 ✉ 236 West 78th Street at Broadway ☎ 212/595-0850 🚇 1, 9 79th Street

SYMPHONY SPACE

Storytelling, readings, children's theater, music, dance and more.

➕ Off map at B4 ✉ 2537 Broadway/95th Street ☎ 212/864-1414 🚇 1, 2, 3, 9 96th Street

Restaurants

PRICES

Prices are approximate, based on a 3-course meal for one person.
$$$ over $60
$$ $40–$60
$ under $40

AIX ($$$)

Didier Virot has brought his own style of robust Provençal cuisine to the Upper West Side at this tri-level restaurant that's always busy. Thyme-citrus smoked brisket and crispy *dorade* with Parmesan crust are typical dishes.

⊞ B5 ⊠ 2398 Broadway/ 88th Street ☎ 212/874-7400 🚇 1, 9 86th Street

BARNEY GREENGRASS ($$)

An Upper West Side tradition since 1929, this is frantic on weekends, when locals feast on huge platters of smoked fish—whitefish, sable, sturgeon and lox—or sandwiches made with similar contents.

⊞ B5 ⊠ 541 Amsterdam Avenue/86th Street ☎ 212/724-4707 🕔 Closed Mon 🚇 1, 9 86th Street

BOAT BASIN CAFÉ ($)

It's hard to find this totally unpretentious place practically on the banks of the Hudson, but if you do, it's worth waiting for a terrace table. The food is dinerlike, without much choice, but you'll be dazzled by the view.

⊞ A6 ⊠ W79th Street/ Hudson River ☎ 212/496-5542 🕔 Closed Mon 🚇 1, 2, 79th Street

CAFÉ DES ARTISTES ($$$)

Howard Chandler Christy murals of frolicking nude nymphs adorn this romantic, art nouveau dining room. The menu is an appealing mix of Hungarian and French dishes, from sturgeon schnitzel to pot au feu.

⊞ B8 ⊠ 1 W67th Street (Central Park West/Columbus Avenue) ☎ 212/877-3500 🚇 1, 9 66th Street

CARMINE'S ($–$$)

Join the mob scene at this mob scene—well, no, it's not actualy anything to do with the Mafia, but this beloved, raucous scene does serve its Sicilian-Italian dishes family-style—huge platters to share. It's not for picky foodies, but it's fun.

⊞ B4 ⊠ 2450 Broadway/ 90th Street ☎ 212/362-2200 🚇 1, 2, 3 96th Street

BRUNCH

It's hard to imagine what New Yorkers did before the invention of brunch. These days the weekend noontime meal can be everything from the basic omelet to a multi-course culinary adventure and it certainly needn't be consumed before noon. A 2pm brunch with mimosas is just fine.

JEAN-GEORGES ($$$)

One of the world's—let alone New York's—great chefs, Alsace native Jean Georges Vongerichten's refined, full-flavored Asian-accented style cannot be imitated. The glass-walled minimalist rooms feel serene and special—perhaps because they were Feng-Shui-ed? Don't miss the molten-center chocolate cake.

⊞ C9 ⊠ Central Park West ☎ 212/299-3900 🚇 A, C, 1, 9, B, C Columbus Circle

OUEST ($$–$$$)

This place single-handedly revitalized the moribund Upper West Side dining scene—it's cozy, yet glamorous with its red booths and the inspired Euro-American posh comfort dishes of chef Tom Valenti. His lamb shanks are legendary.

⊞ B5 ⊠ 2315 Broadway/83rd Street ☎ 212/7995-9559 🚇 1, 2 86th Street

PICHOLINE ($$$)

The Mediterranean cuisine of Terrance Brennan is as good as it ever was at this, his first New York address. Though everybody has got into the cheese act now, this is still the best cart in town (aside from Artisanal).

⊞ C8 ⊠ 35 W64th Street between Central Park West and Broadway ☎ 212/724-8585 🚇 1, 9 66th Street

New York extends far beyond Manhattan and its outer boroughs are increasingly attractive to those who seek a more relaxed approach to life. Brooklyn especially has plenty to engage visitors.

Brooklyn

HIGHLIGHTS

- Smith Street restaurants
- Brooklyn Heights Promenade
- Bandshell concerts
- The Theater and Rose Cinema at BAM
- Ogling houses in the Heights
- The Art Museum

TIP

- Walk across the bridge as dusk is falling in summer and see the sun set behind the Statue of Liberty, and the lights of Manhattan.

Brooklyn has it all—one of the largest art museums in the US and some of New York's best restaurants; beaches and a park; a zoo, aquarium and children's museum; hip neighborhoods and avant-garde arts.

Big, Bigger, Biggest If Brooklyn were still a separate city, it would be the fourth largest in the US. Home to more than 2 million people, it is the most populous of New York's boroughs and the most diverse, with Russian, Middle Eastern, Italian, West Indian, Hasidic Jewish and Chinese neighborhoods. The Brooklyn Museum of Art, intended by McKim, Mead & White to be the biggest museum in the world (it's actually the seventh largest in the US), has collections ranging from pre-Columbian art to 58 Rodin sculptures, plus what many feel

Remsen Street in Brooklyn Heights (left); Brooklyn Bridge seen from Seaport Pier (below)

are the best Egyptian rooms outside the British Museum (and Egypt). With its grand new entrance (opened summer 2004), it abuts Prospect Park—opened in 1867. The Botanic Garden, zoo and the Bandshell summertime events are highlights.

The bridge and beyond With its twin Gothic towers and ballet of cables, the first Manhattan–Brooklyn link fulfills beautifully its symbolic role of affording entry into new worlds of opportunity and the view from here is spectacular. Worth exploring are the established brownstone neighborhoods of Park Slope, Cobble Hill and Brooklyn Heights, the latter famous for the Promenade and its view of Manhattan. Brooklyn Children's Museum, the world's first for kids, has tons to do, including a miniature theater and the "Totally Tots" toddler stamping ground.

THE BASICS

Brooklyn Heights
🚇 2, 3 Clark Street
Brooklyn Museum of Art
✉ 200 Eastern Parkway
☎ 718/638-5000
🕐 Wed–Fri 10–5, Sat–Sun 11–6
🚇 2, 3, Eastern Parkway
Prospect Park
☎ 718/965-8999
🚇 2, 3 Eastern Parkway
Brooklyn Children's Museum
✉ 145 Brooklyn Avenue, Crown Heights
☎ 718/735-4400
🕐 Wed–Fri 2–5, Sat–Sun 10–5
🚇 C Kingston Avenue
💲 Contribution

More to See

BRONX ZOO

The biggest city zoo in the US, 100 years old in 1999, has 4,000 animals, a kid's zoo and monorail. Don't miss the newest attraction, the $43 million Congo Gorilla Forest.

✉ Fordham Road (Bronx River Parkway Northeast) ☎ 718/367-1010 🕐 Apr–end Oct daily 10–5; Nov–end Mar 10–4.30 🍽 Restaurant 🚇 2, 5 Pelham Parkway 💰 Moderate

THE CLOISTERS

A 12th-century Spanish apse attached to a Romanesque cloister and a Gothic chapel—what's all this doing in the Bronx? This is the Met's medieval branch: The incongruity is hallucinogenic and the sights are just heavenly. The collections are arranged chronologically, so you can trace the metamorphosis of architectural styles. The bulk of the art and architecture was amassed by sculptor George Gray Bernard in the early 20th century. Much was rescued from ruin: The effigy of the Crusader Jean d'Alluye, for instance, was doing duty as a bridge,

while the priceless Unicorn Tapestries were acting as frost blankets.

✉ Fort Tryon Park, North Manhattan ☎ 718/923-3700 🕐 Mar–end Oct Tue–Sun 9.30–5.15 ; Nov–end Feb Tue–Sun 9.30–4.45. Closed holidays 🚇 A 190th Street 💰 Moderate

CONEY ISLAND

At the end of the 19th century, Coney Island on a peak day played host to a million people. By 1921 a boardwalk and the subway had arrived, then 1939–40 added the "Parachute jump," now a rusted ghost. The glory days of Luna Park are long since gone, yet seedy Coney Island still draws a crowd. The big-dipper ride, the Cyclone, is still there and Nathan's Famous hot dogs are still sold from the original site. A newer attraction is KeySpan Park, home of the Brookyn Cyclones baseball team. Look out for concerts held here in summer. The New York Aquarium, watery branch of the Bronx Zoo, moved here in 1957. Roughly 10,000 creatures call it home, including beluga whales, coral,

The restful garden at the Cloisters

A Kodiak bear at Bronx Zoo

a penguin colony and five varieties of shark.

✉ Surf Avenue, Boardwalk; Aquarium: W8th Street, Surf Avenue

☎ Sideshow 718/372-5159; KeySpan Park 718/449-8497; Aquarium 718/265–3474

🕐 Aquarium daily 10–5, summer weekends and holidays 10–7 🍽 Cafeteria at Aquarium

Ⓠ W Stillwell Avenue/ Coney Island

✋ Aquarium moderate

QUEENS

The major attractions here are the New York Hall of Science and Queens Museum of Art. The former is a hands-on science and technology museum with a wonderful Science Playground outside for children (✉ 111th Street, Flushing Meadows-Corona Park ☎ 718/699-0005). The art museum (New York Building, Flushing Meadows-Corona Park ☎ 718/592-9700) holds exhibitions of contemporary art, Tiffany glassware and a scale panorama of New York that is regularly updated. Outside stands the Unisphere—the world's largest globe.

STATEN ISLAND

Fine historic sights are housed here. The Alice Austen House (✉ 2 Hylan Boulevard ☎ 718/816-4506) is a museum of photographs by Alice Austen in her Victorian house.

Historic Richmond Town (✉ 441 Clarke Avenue ☎ 718/351-1611) is a restored rural village re-creating the early 19th century.

YANKEE STADIUM

If you want to see what makes the New Yorker tick, go see a Yankees home game. The Yankees dominated the early eras of baseball. In 1920 Babe Ruth joined the team and quickly became a hero. The team had an incredible winning streak when they clinched the World Series title in 1996, 1998, 1999 and 2000.

✉ E161st Street, Bronx ☎ 718/293-4300, Ticketmaster 212/307-1212

🕐 Season runs Apr–end Oct. Check schedule for games

🍽 Concession stands Ⓠ 4, B, D 161st Street ✋ Expensive

Shea Stadium Queens

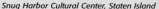

Snug Harbor Cultural Center, Staten Island

Restaurants

AL DI LA ($$)

One of the first food-forward serious restaurants in Brooklyn is still one of the best, as you'll notice as you stand in line (no reservations) or wait in the adjunct wine bar. The food is hearty and Venetian; the look is flea-market chic.

✉ 248 Fifth Avenue/Carroll Street ☎ 718/783-4565 🚇 M, N, R Union Street

BLUE RIBBON ($$)

There's quite a Manhattan feel to this deceptively huge modern-American foodies' favorite, and that's not surprising since it has an older sister there (97 Sullivan Street/ Prince Street, 212/274-0404), beloved by off-duty chefs. The comprehensive menu is perfectly balanced between creativity and comfort.

✉ 280 5th Avenue/1st Street ☎ 718/840-0404 🚇 M, N R Union Street

BUBBY'S ($)

The DUMBO branch of this Tribeca favorite has an identical kitchen serving all-American BLTs, chicken clubs, meat loaf and fries followed (or replaced) by its divine pies but the rest differs enormously—operative word "enormous." Despite its size, expect a stroller jam and a wait at the door for Sunday brunch.

✉ 1 Main Street/ Water Street ☎ 718/222-0666 🚇 F York Street

GROCERY ($$$)

A tiny place with a big reputation, this sweet Carroll Gardens chef-owned place offers constantly changing market-led nouvelle-American menus. Inside is homey, but the lovely tree-shaded garden takes the cake.

✉ 288 Smith Street/Sacket ☎ 718/596-3335 🚇 F, G Carroll Gardens

JUNIOR'S ($)

An institution in a hideous stretch of downtown Brooklyn, this

SHERWOOD CAFÉ

It started out just selling funky French antiques, but the adjunct café grew until it took over entirely. One of the places that kicked the Brooklyn boom into high gear, the place is always packed, for the good French bistro food, the wacky interior and the fairy-tale graveled garden.

✉ 195 Smith Street/ Baltic Street ☎ 718/596-1609 🚇 F, G Bergen Street

two-room diner (the "Café" in back is quieter) is famous for its twin, two-roll, sandwiches and huge portions but, above all, for its creamy cheese-cake in classic New York style.

✉ 386 Flatbush Avenue/DeKalb Avenue ☎ 718/852-5257 🚇 DeKalb Avenue

OSAKA ($$)

Often cited as one of New York's, let alone Brooklyn's, best sushi places, this trendy hole-in-the-wall has some creative maki and salads and a cute wooden-decked garden that more than doubles its size the warm months.

✉ 272 Court Street/Degraw ☎ 718/643-00445 🚇 F, G Bergen Street

PETER LUGER ($$$)

You get steak, some hash browns and creamed spinach for the table, and maybe some tomato-and-onion salad to start—that's it, and that's all you need. It's not about atmosphere or fine wines, its not about feeling special, it's about steak. Since 1887 this landmark has been serving the best beef in New York.

✉ 178 Broadway/Bedford Avenue, Brooklyn ☎ 718/387-7400 🚇 J, M, Z Marcy Avenue

Like all major cities, New York has a range of accommodations from ultratrendy and extravagantly plush to inexpensive B&Bs and chain hotels with plenty in between.

Staying in New York

There are plenty of hotel rooms but it is hard to find a comfortable room under $150. If money is no object, reserve a room at the Carlyle or the Four Seasons.

On a Budget
For less expensive options, check out the inexpensive chains—Red Roof, Super 8 and others. The city also has some B&Bs, less expensive than the average hotel, with good-value extras. Hostels are the least expensive lodging options (see the box below).

Luxury Living
You'll find first-class luxury hotels spread throughout the city, although many are centered in Midtown. Nearly every hotel room comes with air conditioning, private bathroom, cable TV, telephone, coffeemaker, hand hair dryer, but top-class hotel rooms boast luxe fabrics and linens, high-tech electronics, and high staff-to-guest ratios.

Prices
Today there is no such thing as a standard rack rate. Prices fluctuate with customer demand. To get the best rate on a hotel room, call the hotel and ask about the best available rate and special discounts. Alternatively, go online to such discount services as hotels.com, quickbook.com or hoteldiscounts.com. Note that taxes will be added to your bill, plus $2 occupancy tax on a standard room and $4 on a one-bedroom suite.

HOSTELS IN NEW YORK

Big Apple Hostel 119 West 45th, tel 212/302-2603

Chelsea Center Hostel 313 West 29th Street, 10031, tel 212/643-0214

Chelsea International Hostel 251 West 20th Street, tel 212/647-0010

Hostelling International 891 Amsterdam Avenue, tel 212/932-2300

West Side YMCA 5 West 63rd Street, tel 212/875-4100,

Whitehouse 340 Bowery, tel 212/477-5623

Top to bottom: Arriving at the hotel; Peninsula Hotel; doorman at the Ritz-Carlton; Bryant Park hotel

Budget Hotels

PRICES

Expect to pay between $80 and $180 for a budget hotel

CARLTON ARMS

www.carltonarms.com
Decorated with crazy murals, this is perhaps New York's wackiest hotel. Amenities are minimal but there is a communal atmosphere that makes travelers feel at home. As it says on the business card "this ain't no Holiday Inn." 54 rooms.

🚇 F14 ✉ 160 E25th Street ☎ 212/684-8337; 🚇 6 23rd Street

GERSHWIN

www.gershwinhotel.com
"We're just at the edge of hip," says the manager of this first New York Interclub hotel—Urs Jakob's string of super-hostels. Art elevates the style of the 150 basic rooms; bars, roofdecks and lounges encourage sociability.

🚇 E13 ✉ 7 E27th Street ☎ 212/545-8000 🍴 Café 🚇 N, R 23rd Street

HOTEL BELLECLAIRE

www.hotelbelleclaire.com
Mark Twain lived here, as well as Maxim Gorky. Now the early-20th-century building offers 167 clean, minimal guest rooms, with pine furniture and pale apricot-color walls though only the shared-bathroom rooms

are budget rate.
🚇 B6 ✉ 250 W77th Street ☎ 212/362-7700; fax: 212/362-1004 🚇 1, 9 79th Street

HOTEL 17

www.hotel17ny.com
The décor is so kitschily awful it almost looks deliberate—its no-style stripey wallpaper, floral bedspread, nylon carpet look seems to hit a chord with rock and roll types and models. That could also be on account of its brownstone New York Gramercy Park location and its dirt cheap rates.

🚇 F15 ✉ 225 E17th Street (2nd/3rd Avenues) ☎ 212/475-2845 🚇 L 3rd Avenue

HOTEL QT

www.hotelqt.com
Hot hotelier Andre Balazs's first budget hotel has been in every shelter magazine—but don't get too excited: the off-lobby

B&BS

Those who prefer real neighborhoods, authentic experiences and behaving like a local may opt for a B&B. Often these are found in Brooklyn brownstones, where the host has an extra room. Others are empty apartments. The only imperative is to reserve ahead. Another ever-more-popular option is to check the sublet vacation rentals and housing swap listings at www.craigslist.org

exhibitionists' swimming pool and other such high-design features are mostly found in the public areas. Rooms, however, do have nice bedlinens, flatscreen TVs and Wi-Fi. It's meant for—and is attracting—the young.

🚇 C10 ✉ 125 W45th Street ☎ 212/566-1900 🚇 A, C Chambers Street

OLCOTT

A much-loved New York address for many performing artists, thanks to its Lincoln Center proximity and reasonable rates. The Olcott's 150 rooms are mostly suites, complete with kitchenettes and often a separate living room with TV. It's shabby but homey. Three-night minimum stay.

🚇 B7 ✉ 27 W72nd Street ☎ 212/877-4200 🚇 1, 2, 3, 9 72nd Street

WASHINGTON SQUARE

www.washingtonsquarehotel.com
This is the only hotel in the heart of Greenwich Village. Amenities are minimal—deliberately so, to keep the rates down, but the place still manages to be almost chic. 165 rooms.

🚇 E16 ✉ 103 Waverley Place ☎ 212/777-9515 🍴 CIII 🚇 1, 9 Christopher Street

Mid-Range Hotels

PRICES

Expect to pay between $180 and $350 for a mid-range hotel

BEEKMAN TOWER

www.affinia.com
The art deco tower in far-east Midtown has a lot going for it: well-kept rooms and suites, some with kitchens, most larger than the average with somewhat fusty but comfy furnishings, a fitness center, room service and two restaurants including the 26th-story Top of the Tower, with great river and city views.
➕ G10 ✉ 3 Mitchell Place/1st Avenue ☎ 212/355-7300 🚇 6 51st Street

THE BENJAMIN

www.thebenjamin.com
Rooms in this environmentally conscious Midtown 1920s block have a sophisticatred neutral palette, excellent work areas with printer/faxes and beds with Frette sheets, down duvets and pillows you select from a menu. Caring service, plus a spa, fitness center, room service, restaurant and wine bar all adds up to an excellent value.
➕ E10 ✉ 125 E50th Street/Park Avenue ☎ 212/715-2500 🚇 1, 2, 3 72nd Street

CHELSEA HOTEL

www.hotelchelsea.com
The legendary dive actually does remain a hotel, though about half of it houses residents of the louche, trendsetting, rock and roll kind. As for the rooms for hire, shabby chic doesn't begin to capture the faded—*very* faded— grandeur of the big ones; small ones are functional at best and housekeeping is hit or miss. Only consider this if you already know and love the place's history.
➕ C14 ✉ 222 W23rd Street/7th Avenue ☎ 212/243-3700 🚇 1, 2 7th Avenue

COSMOPOLITAN

www.cosmohotel.com
No frills in any sense of the word exist at this 105-room, seven-story block in Tribeca. But, if you find the real estate rule applies to hotels, you'll love it—the location, location, location is prime. The clean, fully functional rooms vary a good deal in size, so if they're not full and you're not happy, ask to see another.
➕ E20 ✉ 95 W Broadway/Chambers Street ☎ 212/566-1900 🚇 A, C Chambers Street

EXCELSIOR

www.excelsiorhotelny.com
The location is quite fabulous, steps from Central Park and the American Museum of Natural History, with the subway practically underfoot, and the building is grand, too, heavy on the wood paneling, faux-oils and gilt frames. Rooms, though not beautiful in the generic brocades and stripes, are fine; some standard ones even overlook the park.
➕ C6 ✉ 45 W81st Street/Central Park West ☎ 212/362-9200 🚇 B, C 81st Street/Museum of Natural History

HOTEL BEACON

www.beaconhotel.com
In the middle of Broadway, on the Upper West Side, the Beacon feels more like an apartment building than a hotel. Some of the 200-plus rooms have kitchenettes.
➕ B7 ✉ 2130 Broadway (75th Street) ☎ 212/787-1100 🚇 1, 2, 3 72nd Street

THE ALGONQUIN

The Algonquin is forever associated with the only group of literary wits to be named after a piece of furniture: the Algonquin Round Table. The bon viveurs achieved almost as much at the bar here as they did in the pages of the embryo *New Yorker*, with Robert Benchley, Dorothy Parker and Alexander Woolcott well ensconced. The hotel's Rose Room still contains the very table they occupied.
www.algonquinhotel.com

THE HUDSON
www.hudsonhotel.com
Ian Schrager's fourth New York address has 1,000 rooms and all the expected accoutrements. There is the Hudson Bar, complete with glowing yellow dance floor and outside courtyard, plus a gym with a pool, bowling alley and archery. The mirror-and-mahogany-walled rooms are small.
⊞ C9 ✉ 356 W58th Street ☎ 212/554-6000 🍴 Hudson Cafeteria 🚇 A, B, C, D, 1, 9 Columbus Circle

MARITIME HOTEL
www.themaritimehotel.com
Heat-seeking trendsters will love this quirky 120-room place in the thick of the Meatpacking District. Porthole windows facing the Hudson conceal small rooms with a ship-like feel and navy-blue soft furnishings. Fitness center, happening bar scene and Japanese restaurant.
⊞ C15 ✉ 363 W16th Street/9th Avenue ☎ 212/242-4300 🍴 Matsuri 🚇 A, C, E 14th Street

OFF SOHO SUITES
www.offsoho.com
Since this place opened a few years ago its very off-Soho location on the Lower East Side bordering Nolita has become all the rage. The suites are mini-studio apartments with no decorative advantages whatsoever but with full kitchens, private phones and satellite TV.

"Economy" suites share kitchen and bathroom.
⊞ F18 ✉ 11 Rivington Street/Bowery ☎ 212/979-9808 🚇 F 2nd Avenue; J, M Bowery

70 PARK AVENUE
www.70parkavenuehotel.com
The first foray into New York by boutique hotel pioneers Kimpton, this 205-room Murray Hill place has a quietly contemporary décor, extras like touch-screen room service, pillow menu, good sound systems and a special yoga channel on the huge flatscreen TV.
⊞ E12 ✉ 70 Park Avenue/38th Street ☎ 212/973-2400 🍴 Silverleaf Tavern 🚇 4, 5, 6, 7, S Grand Central Station 42nd Street

THE SHOREHAM
www.shorehamhotel.com
The sleek Shoreham

LIBRARY
Each floor of the hotel is dedicated to a subject category from the Dewey Decimal system and each room has a collection of art and books related to a subcategory. The interior is modern and minimalist. Amenities include multiline phones with high-speed internet access.
www.libraryhotel.com
✉ 299 Madison Avenue ☎ 212/983-4500 🚇 S, 4, 5 6 7 Gand Central/42nd Streets

---

Hotel, behind the Museum of Modern Art has 174 small but cozy rooms, with ultra-suede walls, diffused lighting and puffy white comforters on the beds. The choice rooms are in the back. Extras such as Aveda products, free round-the-clock cappuccino and espresso and a hotel-curated art gallery, plus high-end electronics (Bose Wave, plasma screens, XBox 360s) in the better rooms add value.
⊞ D10 ✉ 33 W55th Street ☎ 212/247-6700 🍴 La Caravelle 🚇 B, Q 57th Street

THE TIME
www.thetimenycom
Just off Times Square, this place has really gone to town on the wacky décor: Choose a red, yellow or blue room and you'll find that color not only covering the bed and selected wall parts but also appearing in candy and scent form. A Bose radio and Molton Brown toiletries add value but can't make the small rooms grow any larger, though you can spread out a bit in the small gym and rather swank lounge and restaurant.
⊞ C11 ✉ 224 W49th Street/8th Avenue ☎ 212/246-5252 🚇 N, Q, R, S, W, 1, 2, 3, 7, 42nd Street

Luxury Hotels

PRICES

Expect to pay from $350 for a luxury hotel

FOUR SEASONS
www.fourseasons.com
The grandiose I. M. Pei building makes a big first impression—all towering lobbies, marble and mezzanine lounges. And the rooms don't disappoint. In beiges and creams; they're big, with tons of closets, tubs that fill in no time and, in some, great views. Many consider this Manhattan's top hotel.
🔰 E9 ✉ 57 E57th Street, Midtown East ☎ 212/758-570 🍴 5757 🚇 B, Q 57th Street

HOTEL GANSEVOORT
www.hotelgansevoort.com
You see the illuminated glass tower for blocks. The fashion-obsessed young creatives who consider this area style-central populate the stark rooms with their stone and sand colors and high-tech everything, and also the popular Ono restaurant and its O Bar. The rooftop pool is a major plus.
🔰 C16 ✉ 18 9th Avenue/13th Street ☎ 212/206-6700 🚇 A, C, E, L 14th Street

MANDARIN ORIENTAL
www.mandarinoriental.com
This chain is known for its clean lines, its fabulous spas and its service. The best of the 251 rooms have panoramic views.
🔰 C9 ✉ 80 Columbus Circle/60th Street ☎ 212/399-3938 🍴 Asiate 🚇 A, B, C, D, 1, 9 59th Street Columbus Circle

MERCER HOTEL
www.mercerhotel.com
André Balazs was the first to do hip hotels that care about more than looks and this one, in central Soho, is a perfect example. The Christian Liaigre design is cool and calm; the rooms are huge (mostly) and sexy; the lobby, bar and basement restaurant attract locals as much as visitors.
🔰 E18 ✉ 147 Mercer Street/Prince Street ☎ 212/966- 6060 🍴 Mercer Kitchen 🚇 N, R Prince Street

RITZ-CARLTON BATTERY PARK
www.ritzcarlton.com
This glass-sided tower has one thing no other hotel has: the harbor. Decor in the rooms-with-everything is pale and contemporary, and the service and facilities are exemplary.
🔰 D23 ✉ 2 West Street/Battery Place ☎ 212/344-0800 🚇 1, 2 South Ferry

ST. REGIS
www.starwood.com/stregis
Formal Louis XV style in the middle of Midtown. The service is discreet, and the 221 rooms and 92 suites are plush.
🔰 E9–E10 ✉ 2 E55th Street at 5th/Madison Avenues ☎ 212/753-4500 🚇 6 51st Street

60 THOMPSON
www.60thompson.com
Fashionista boutique hotel in Soho with 100 sleekly contemporary rooms in textural neutrals. Most bathrooms have only showers. The rooftop bar/lounge, A60, with restricted access for outsiders is ever so glamorous as is the Thai restaurant, Kittichai, and the bar, Thom.
🔰 D18 ✉ 60 Thompson Street/Broome ☎ 877/431-0400 🚇 A, C, E Canal Street

THE STYLE OF LUXURY

In the last two decades a crop of ultra-chic hotels opened around the city that offer guests truly luxurious amenities in modern, stylish settings. The first was the Royalton, which started the trend in 1987. A steady trickle followed… then the deluge. The hotels not only offer hip accommodations and grand services, but also restaurants, lounges and bars that attract trendy New Yorkers from all corners of the city.

Use this section to help you plan your visit to New York. We have suggested the best ways to get around the city and useful information for while you are there.

Planning Ahead

When to Go

Fall is generally thought the best time to visit New York. In August many New Yorkers are driven out of town by the searing heat. However, during this time lines are shorter, restaurant reservations optional and outdoor festivals at their peak. The city has occasional blizzards in winter, but these rarely cause disruption.

AVERAGE DAILY MAXIMUM TEMPERATURES

JAN	FEB	MAR	APR	MAY	JUN	JUL	AUG	SEP	OCT	NOV	DEC
39°F	41°F	46°F	61°F	70°F	81°F	84°F	82°F	77°F	66°F	54°F	39°F
4°C	5°C	8°C	16°C	21°C	27°C	29°C	28°C	25°C	19°C	12°C	4°C

Spring (March to May) is unpredictable—even in April snow showers can alternate with shirtsleeves weather—but the worst of winter is over by mid-March.
Summer (June to August) can be extremely hot and humid, especially July and August.
Fall (September to November) sees warm temperatures persisting into October.
Winter (December to February) can be severe, with heavy snow, biting winds and subfreezing temperatures.

WHAT'S ON

January/February *Chinese New Year* (Chinatown).
March 17 *St. Patrick's Day Parade* (5th Avenue, 44th–86th Streets).
March/April *Easter Parade* (5th Avenue, 44th–59th Streets).
April–October *Baseball*
May *9th Avenue International Food Festival* (9th Avenue, 37th–57th Streets ☎ 800/894-9166).
Martin Luther King Day Parade (3rd Sun 5th Avenue, 44th–86th Streets).
June *Metropolitan Opera park concerts* (☎ 212/362-6000).
JVC Jazz Festival (various

venues ☎ 212/501-1390).
Lesbian and Gay Pride Parade (5th Avenue, Midtown to Washington Square).
July 4 *Independence Day*
July–August *Shakespeare in the Park* (Delacorte Theater ☎ 212/539-8655).
NY Philharmonic park concerts (☎ 212/875-5709).
August *Harlem Week* (☎ 212/862-8477).
August–September *Lincoln Center Out-of-Doors Festival* (☎ 212/875-5108).
US Open Tennis Championships (☎ 718/760-6200).

September *Feast of San Gennaro* (Little Italy).
September–October *New York Film Festival* (Lincoln Center ☎ 212/875-5050).
Columbus Day Parade (Fifth Avenue, 44th–86th streets).
November *NYC Marathon* (Staten Island to Central Park ☎ 212/423-2249).
Macy's Thanksgiving Day Parade (✉ Central Park West, 81st Street ☎ 212/494-4495).
December Tree Lighting Ceremony (✉ Rockefeller Center ☎ 212/632-3975).
New Year's Eve celebrations (✉ Times Square).

New York City Online

www.livebroadway.com

Live Broadway offers up-to-the-minute details on show times and tickets, as well as reviews.

http://newyork.citysearch.com

City Search has links to and listings for attractions, entertainment, restaurants, shopping, hotels and more. Also has news, reviews and a directory offering NYC information.

www.nyc.gov

As the official homepage of the City of New York, the site offers links to the Office of the Mayor as well as information about community services, legal policies, city agencies, news and weather.

www.ny.com

Billing itself as "the paperless guide to New York City," ny.com's "How, Wow and Now" sections let you know what's up on New York's entertainment, dining and nightlife scene. Sports section lists professional events.

www.nysale.com

Information on sample sales, showroom sales, warehouse sales and clearance sales.

www.nytimes.com

Here you'll get an inside look at one of the world's most respected newspapers. The site has links to sections covering everything from world affairs to sports and local gossip.

www.nycvisit.com

The official tourism website. Includes calendar of events, accommodations information, updates on laws, transit and lots more.

www.timessquare.com

All about Times Square and the area around, Broadway and its theaters in particular; with booking information.

PRIME TRAVEL SITES

www.fodors.com
A complete travel-planning site. You can research prices and weather; book air tickets, cars and rooms; pose questions to fellow travelers and find links to other sites.

www.iloveny.com
Official NY State site. Information about touring the region.

www.mta.info
Metropolitan Transportation Authority updates you on service changes and disruptions, and answers questions about buses and subway.

INTERNET CAFÉS

Cybercafé
✉ 250 W49th Street
(Broadway/8th Avenue)
☎ 212/333-4109
🕐 Mon–Fri 8am–11pm, Sat and Sun 1–11

Kinko's have locations throughout the city, many open 24 hours.
☎ 800-2-KINKOS

Starbucks now provide wireless hookups, a service that is proliferating in the city.

Getting There

ENTRY REQUIREMENTS

Visitors to New York from outside the US must have a full passport and a return ticket. For countries participating in the Visa Waiver Program, a visa is not required, though you must fill out the green visa-waiver form issued on the plane. You are also required to fill out a customs form and an immigration form.

FROM LA GUARDIA

The journey to Manhattan takes between 45 and 60 minutes. SuperShuttle runs a shared minibus 8am–11pm (cost $15–$20). Services to Manhattan are also provided by New York Airport Service Express (cost $10–23). Taxis cost $25–$45, plus tolls and tip.

ARRIVING BY LAND

● Greyhound buses from across the US and Canada and commuter buses from New Jersey arrive at the Port Authority Terminal (✉ 42nd Street at 8th Avenue ☎ 212/564-8484).
● Commuter trains use Grand Central Terminal (✉ 42nd Street at Park Avenue ☎ 212/532-4900). Long-distance trains arrive at Pennsylvania Station (✉ 31st Street at 8th Avenue ☎ 212/582-6875).

AIRPORTS

New York has three airports–John F. Kennedy (✉ Queens, 15 miles/24km east of Manhattan ☎ 718/244-444), Newark (✉ New Jersey, 16 miles/25km west ☎ 973/961-6000) and La Guardia (✉ Queens, 8 miles/13km east ☎ 718/533-3400). Most international flights arrive at J.F.K.

18 MILES (29KM)

La Guardia Airport
8 miles (13km) to city center Bus/minibus 45–60 minutes, $15

J.F.K. Airport
15 miles (24km) to city center Bus/minibus 1 hour, $13–22

Newark Airport
16 miles (25km) to city center Bus/minibus 40 minutes, $12–19

FROM J.F.K.

The journey to Manhattan takes around an hour, depending on traffic. New York Airport Service Express Bus (☎ 718/875-8200) runs every 15–30 minutes, 6.15am–10.11pm ($15). The SuperShuttle (☎ 800/258-3826) runs to Manhattan 24 hours a day ($17–$20). To reserve, use the courtesy telephone next to the Ground Transportation Desk. A free shuttle bus runs to the A train. Taxis costs $45 plus tolls; use the official taxi stand. The AirTrain to Jamaica (E.J.Z. subway and Long Island Railroad) or Howard Beach (A subway) costs $5 and takes 12 minutes, plus 60–90 minutes to midtown.

FROM NEWARK

It takes about 60 minutes to Manhattan. AirTrain (☎ 888/397-4636) goes direct from all terminals to Penn Station (A, C, E, 1, 2, 3 subway); follow signs to Monorail/AirTrain. SuperShuttle (☎ 212/315-3006) runs a minibus to Midtown 7am–11pm ($15–20). A taxi costs about $55, plus tolls and a $15 surcharge from Manhattan.

Getting Around

BUSES

● Bus stops are on or near corners, marked by a sign and a yellow painted curb. Any ride costs the same as the subway and you can use a Metrocard or correct change ($2).

● Bus maps are available from token booth clerks in subway stations.

● Buses are safe, clean and excruciatingly slow. The fastest are Limited Stop buses.

● Ask the driver for a transfer that entitles you to a free onward or crosstown journey for an hour after boarding using the intersecting services listed on the back.

● A bus map is essential.

SUBWAY

● New York's subway system has 26 routes and 468 stations, many open 24 hours (those with a green globe outside are always staffed).

● To ride the subway you need a Metrocard, which you can refill. Unlimited ride Metrocards are also available; with these you must wait 18 minutes between swipes. Swipe the card to enter the turnstile.

● Many stations have separate entrances for up- and downtown services. Make sure you take a local train, not a restricted-stop express.

● Cars are air-conditioned in summer. There is often some service outage that is announced on notices in the stations and on the MTA website.

● Children under 44in (113cm) tall ride free.

● Transit information ☎ 718/330-1234
◉ 6am–10pm; www.mta.info

● Avoid the less populated subway lines at night. If you do ride at night, stay in the "off hour waiting area" until your train arrives.

TAXIS

● A yellow cab is vacant when the central number on the roof is illuminated and the "Off Duty" side lights are not.

● All cabs display current rates on the door, have a meter inside and can supply a printed receipt.

LOST PROPERTY

● You are unlikely to recover lost items but try the following:

Subway and bus
☎ 718/625-6200

Taxi
☎ 212/840-4734

J.F.K.
☎ 718/656-4120

Newark
☎ 201/961-2230

You should report any loss as soon as possible if you plan to claim on your insurance.

SUBWAY TIPS

● If your Metrocard didn't work, don't go to a different turnstile or you'll lose a fare. As the display says, you should "swipe again."

● Check the circular signs on the outside of the cars to make sure you're boarding the correct train. Often two lines share a platform.

● Look at the boards above your head to check whether you're on the Up- or Downtown side and/or on the Local or Express track.

BROOKLYN

If you're visiting friends or sights in Brooklyn, the same subway rules apply, but you may have to change trains since several local lines (1, 6, E, V, W) only operate in Manhattan (not Queens). No buses cross the bridges but you can pick up a Brooklyn bus map at subway stations.

VISITORS WITH DISABILITIES

City law requires that all facilities constructed after 1987 provide complete access to people with disabilities. Many owners of older buildings have willingly added disability-access features as well. Two important resources for travelers with disabilities are the Mayor's Office for People with Disabilities (✉ 100 Gold Street, second floor ☎ 212/788-2830) and Hospital Audiences' guide to New York's cultural institutions, called *Access for All* (☎ 212/575-7660). This $5 book describes the accessibility of each place and includes information on hearing and visual aids, alternative entrances and the height of telephones and water fountains. H.A. also provides descriptions of theater performances on audio cassettes for people with visual impairments.

- Cab drivers are notorious for (a) knowing nothing about New York geography, (b) not speaking English and (c) having an improvisational driving style.
- Tip at least 15 percent. Bills larger than $10 are unpopular for short journeys.

DRIVING

- Driving in New York is not recommended, but a car is essential for excursions further afield.
- The address of the nearest major car-rental outlet can be found by calling the following toll-free numbers:

Avis ☎ 800/331-1212;
Budget ☎ 800/527-0700;
Hertz ☎ 800/654-3080;
Thrifty ☎ 800/367-2277

- If driving in New York is unavoidable, make sure you understand the restrictions because penalties for infringements are stringent.
- In many streets parking alternates daily from one side to the other and it is illegal to park within 10ft (3m) either side of a fire hydrant. A car illegally parked will be towed away and the driver heavily fined.
- Within the city limits right turns at a red light are prohibited and the speed limit is 30mph (48kph).
- Passing a stopped school bus is illegal and stiff fines can be imposed.

WALKING

New York is one of the few US cities in which the predominant mode of transportation is the foot. Especially if the weather is cooperating (and if it isn't, umbrella vendors materialize on every other corner), it's far nicer to hike a 10- or 20-block distance than to descend below ground on the subway, or sit in a cab stalled in traffic. It's also often faster. To work it out for yourself, figure one minute per short block (north–south) and two per long block (east–west, on cross streets). New Yorkers tend to walk fast and there are few collisions.

Essential Facts

CUSTOMS
● Non-US citizens may import duty-free:
1 quart (just under a liter) of alcohol (no one under 21 can import alcohol), 200 cigarettes or 50 cigars and $100 of gifts.
● Have a doctor's certificate for any medication you are taking with you.
● Among restricted items for import are meat, fruit, plants, seeds and lottery tickets.

ELECTRICITY
● The supply is 100 volts, 60 cycles AC current.
● US appliances use two-prong plugs.
European appliances require an adapter.

ETIQUETTE
● Tipping: waitstaff get 15–20 percent (roughly double the 8.25 percent sales tax at the bottom of the bill); so do cab drivers. Bartenders get about the same (though less than $1 is stingy). Bellhops ($1 per bag), room service waiters (10 percent), and hairdressers (15–20 percent) should also be tipped.
● There are stringent smoking laws in New York. Smoking is banned on all public transportation, in cabs and in all places of work, including restaurants and bars.

MEDICAL TREATMENT
● It is essential to have adequate insurance.
● In the event of an emergency, the 911 operator will send an ambulance.
● Doctors on Call (24 hours)
☎ 212/737–2333
● Near Midtown, 24-hour emergency rooms:
St. Luke's-Roosevelt Hospital ✉ 58th Street (9th Avenue) ☎ 212/523-6800
St. Vincent's Hospital ✉ Seventh Avenue /11th Street ☎ 212/604-7997
● Dental Emergency Service ☎ 212/679-3966, after 8pm 212/679-4172

MEDICINES
● Several drugstores are open 24 hours.

VISITOR INFORMATION
● NYC & Company provides free bus and subway maps, calendars of events and discount coupons for Broadway shows ✉ 810 7th Avenue ☎ 212/484-1222 🕓 Mon–Fri 9–6, weekends 8.30–5
● There are also information booths at City Hall Park ✉ Broadway and Park Row 🕓 Mon–Fri 9–6, Sat–Sun 10–6 and Harlem, Adam Clayton Powell State Office Building Plaza ✉ 163 W125th Street (7th Avenue) 🕓 Mon–Fri 9–6, Sat–Sun 10–6

EMERGENCY NUMBERS
● Police, Fire Department, Ambulance ☎ 911
● Police, Fire Department, Ambulance for the deaf ☎ 800/342-4357
● Crime Victims Hotline ☎ 212/577-7777
● Sex Crimes Report Line ☎ 212/267-7273

TOILETS
● Don't use public toilets on the street, in stations or in subways.
● Public buildings provide locked bathrooms (ask the doorman, cashier or receptionist for the key).
● Otherwise, use toilets in hotel lobbies, bars or restaurants.

MONEY

The unit of currency is the dollar (=100 cents). Notes (bills) come in denominations of $1, $5, $10, $20, $50 and $100; coins come in 25¢ (a quarter), 10¢ (a dime), 5¢ (a nickel) and 1¢ (a penny).

5 dollars

10 dollars

50 dollars

100 dollars

VISA AND TRAVEL INSURANCE

Check your insurance coverage and buy a supplementary policy if needed. A minimum of $1 million medical cover is recommended. Choose a policy that also includes trip cancellation, baggage and document loss.

MONEY MATTERS

● Credit cards are widely accepted. Visa, MasterCard, American Express, Diner's Card and Discover are most commonly used.
● Traveler's checks are accepted but are rarely seen. Don't bother trying to exchange these at the bank—fees are high.

NEWSPAPERS AND MAGAZINES

● The local papers are the *New York Times* (with a huge Sunday edition), the *Daily News* (also with a generously supplemented Sunday edition) and the *New York Post*. Also look for the respected *Wall Street Journal* and the pink-hued, gossip-heavy, weekly *New York Observer*.
● As well as the *New Yorker, New York* and *Time Out New York*, you may also see the self-conciously hip *The Paper*, the glossy *Manhattan File* and the even glossier *Avenue*.

OPENING HOURS

● Banks: Mon–Fri 9–3 or 3.30; some are open longer, and on Saturday.
● Stores: Mon–Sat 10–6; many are open far later, and on Sunday; those in the Villages, Nolita and SoHo open and close later.
● Museums: hours vary, but Monday is the most common closing day.
● Post offices: Mon–Fri 10–5 or 6.

MAIL AND TELEPHONES

● The main post office ⊠ 8th Avenue (33rd Street) ☎ 212/967-8585 is open 24 hours. Branch post offices are listed in Yellow Pages ⏰ Mon–Fri 8–6, Sat 8–1
● Stamps are also available from hotel concierges, online at www.usps.com, at some delis and from vending machines in stores.
● All New York numbers require the prefix to be dialed (212, 718, 646 or 917). As with all long-distance calls, add a "1" before the code.
● Hotels can levy hefty surcharges, even on local calls, so use payphones instead or the long-distance services of AT&T, MCI and Sprint;

typically, you dial an 800 number.
● Prepaid phonecards are widely available in stores, and there are a few credit card phones.
● To call the US from the UK, dial 001. To call the UK from the US, dial 011 44, then drop the first zero from the area code.

SENSIBLE PRECAUTIONS
● Maintain awareness of your surroundings and of other people, and try to look as though you know your way around.
● Don't get involved with street crazies, however entertaining they are.
● The less populated subway lines are best avoided at night and also certain areas of Brooklyn. Generally, areas of Manhattan that were once considered unsafe (Alphabet City east of Avenue C, the far west of Midtown, north of about 110th Street and Central Park) are far less edgy than they used to be. Still, keep your wits about you in deserted areas.
● Use common-sense rules: conceal your wallet; keep the fastener of your bag on the inside; don't let your handbag dangle over the back of your chair; and don't flash large amounts of cash or jewelry.
● New York women are streetwise and outspoken, so if you are a woman and someone's bugging you, tell him to get lost—he'll be expecting it.

RADIO AND TELEVISION
● New York's National Public Radio station, WNYC, broadcasts avant-garde and classical music, as well as jazz, news and cultural shows on FM 93.9 and AM 820.
● Air America's (WL1B1190 AM) *Al Franken Show* and *Majority Report* with comedian Janeane Garofalo reflect New York's liberal bias, as does Comedy Central's hit *The Daily Show* with Jon Stewart on cable TV.

STUDENTS
● An International Student Identity Card (ISIC) is good for reduced admission at many museums, theaters and other attractions.
● Carry the ISIC or some other photo ID card at all times, to prove you're over 21
● Under-25s will find it hard to rent a car.

CONSULATES

Australia	✉ 636 5th Avenue ☎ 212/245-4000
Canada	✉ 1251 6th Avenue ☎ 212/586-2400
Denmark	✉ 825 3rd Avenue ☎ 212/223-4545
France	✉ 934 5th Avenue ☎ 212/606-3600
Germany	✉ 460 Park Avenue ☎ 212/308-8700
Ireland	✉ 515 Madison Avenue ☎ 212/319-2555
Italy	✉ 690 Park Avenue ☎ 212/737-9100
Netherlands	✉ 1 Rockefeller Plaza ☎ 212/249-1429
Norway	✉ 825 3rd Avenue ☎ 212/421-7333
Sweden	✉ Dag Hammarskjøld Plaza ☎ 212/751-5900
UK	✉ 845 3rd Avenue ☎ 212/752-8400

Timeline

THE FIGHT FOR INDEPENDENCE

In 1664 Wall Street's wall failed to deter the British, who invaded Manhattan Island and named it New York. Almost 100 years later, in 1763, the Treaty of Paris gave the British control over 13 American colonies. In 1770 the Sons of Liberty fought the British at the Battle of Golden Hill and in 1776 the American Revolutionary War began and the British chose New York as their headquarters. The Declaration of Independence was read at Bowling Green in July 1776 and the Treaty of Paris ended the war in 1783.

Pre–1600 New York is populated by Native American groups.

1609 Henry Hudson sails up the Hudson seeking the North West Passage.

1625 "Nieuw Amsterdam" is founded by the Dutch West India Company. A year later the colony's leader buys Manhattan Island from the Native Americans for $24 of trinkets.

1664 The British invade.

1776 American Revolutionary War begins.

1783 War ends. Two years later New York becomes capital of the United States.

1789 George Washington is sworn in as first US president at Federal Hall.

1790 Philadelphia becomes US capital.

1807 Robert Fulton launches his first steamboat, creating trade routes that make many New Yorkers' fortunes.

1827 Slavery in New York is abolished.

1848 Start of first great immigrant waves.

1861 New York backs the Union during the Civil War.

1868 The first "El" (elevated train) opens.

1886 The Statue of Liberty is unveiled.

1892 Ellis Island opens.

1904 New York's first subway opens.

1929 The Great Depression begins.

1933 Prohibition ends. Fiorello La Guardia becomes mayor.

1954 Ellis Island is closed down.

1964 Race riots in Harlem and Brooklyn.

1975 A federal loan saves New York City from bankruptcy.

1990 David Dinkins, New York's first black mayor, takes office.

2001 Terrorists fly two hijacked passenger planes into the World Trade Center twin towers, destroying them and killing an estimated 3,000 people.

2002 Rudy Giuliani's term as mayor ends. Michael Bloomberg takes office.

2004 New Yorkers vote overwhelmingly for presidential candidate John Kerry. President George W. Bush begins second term.

2006 FBI uncovers a plot to attack New York's subway. Terrorists arrested.

TENEMENT LIFE

As you make your first explorations in New York, consider how it was for the early immigrants, especially those who were herded through Ellis Island, then crammed into Lower East Side tenements. Imagine how daunting the cast iron-framed SoHo buildings must have appeared to someone from, say, Vienna. Although they are now the scene of costly loft living, or home to chain stores or swank boutiques, during the immigrant boom they were sweatshop skyscrapers—symbols of hope for a fresh future.

An early view of the Bay of New York (far left); Customs House, New York (left); Brooklyn Bridge in the 19th century (below right); modern-day transportation on the subway (below)

Index